The great news about this book is that you really get the sense that you're being drawn to an encounter with Jesus and where He's inviting us to go. I must say that in the midst of so much chatter and theorizing about the current state of affairs in "the church," we are not merely being fed another perspective or opinion here. This is beyond refreshing—it's actually quite radical. Paul brings a much needed perspective as we wrestle with re-discovering Christian community that is grounded in real life and engaged with the culture at large. Maybe we should wonder—was Jesus ever in the building at all?

— DAVID RUIS

SINGER, MUSICIAN AND SONGWRITER;
FOUNDER, BASILEA COMMUNITY

In *Jesus Has Left the Building*, Paul Vieira graciously and generously points the way to new vistas where God is taking His beloved community in our postmodern context. With the divine sensitivity of a prophet and the heart of a teacher, we are shown how following Jesus in the twenty-first century strongly echoes the ancient rhythms of the very first century.

— MIKE MORRELL

ZOECARNATE.COM

Yes, *Jesus Has Left The Building,* for God has always moved in and *beyond* religion. You will be encouraged by Paul's transparency as he wrestles to the heart of the Gospel uncovering a way of experiencing Jesus beyond our best expectations.

— JONATHAN CAMPBELL, PhD,
CO-AUTHOR OF *THE WAY OF JESUS*

This book has been a blessing and a challenge to me! Having known Paul for nearly 20 years, I can testify personally to the pilgrimage he has made. As I generally minister outside of the ongoing discussion regarding post-structural Christianity, I appreciate all the more the insights of *Jesus Has Left the Building.* Paul's thinking is clearly based on Scripture, yet informed by his own trials and tribulations. But you will find no navel-gazing or pent up bitterness toward the Church here! Paul's love for the Body of Christ leaves an indelible imprint on the reader, but not as much as his love for God. This refreshing work tackles with unstinting commitment the issues facing all genuine disciples of Christ who want to serve God's agendas more effectively in today's world.

— JASON MANDRYK

CO-AUTHOR OF *OPERATION WORLD*

"Jesus Has Left The Building." In fact, He probably never really wanted to be "in" it in the first place. From Exodus 19 onwards it is clear that God's intention for His people was that they be a kingdom of priests; that each one of us impact our world, our sphere of influence, and not just gather together to bless each other. And based on the latest research from the Barna Organization, it is not just Jesus who has left the building. Increasingly, Christians by the millions are opting for more effective ways to serve the Lord together. In this fascinating study, Paul helps us understand from both scripture and his personal journey why this is happening and what the Lord is doing in helping His people re-engage with their world.

— TONY DALE

EDITOR OF *HOUSE2HOUSE MAGAZINE*

JESUS HAS LEFT THE BUILDING

BY

PAUL VIEIRA

JESUS HAS LEFT THE BUILDING

Copyright © 2006 Paul Vieira

ISBN: 0-9718040-8-7

Cover design: Aaron Deckler www.lolight.com
Author Photo: Mark Humphries

Some of the anecdotal illustrations in this book are true to life and are included with the permission of the persons involved. All other illustrations are composites of real situations, and any resemblance to people living or dead is coincidental.

To my devoted wife Tamara.

You arrived before me.

Thank you for your patience.

TABLE OF CONTENTS

Table Of Contents

ACKNOWLEDGMENTS

Writing, editing, and publishing this book has been an amazing journey. I could not have done this alone.

I thank God for friends in Winnipeg who have walked this path with me. We have laughed together for freedom's sake. We have wept together over the price of that freedom. I think of the many hours and years that we have spent talking, praying, and thinking through the implications of our steps. This book is yours as well.

I am also so grateful for the precious people whom I have had the privilege of meeting in my travels. My dear friends from Bermuda, Chicago, Indiana, Iowa, Ohio, Minnesota, and Wisconsin...you know who you are. You showed me that this is bigger than I thought.

Then there are the people who read my manuscript and made it better. Thank you Mark, Matthew, Jules, and Chaelee.

Finally, I want to thank Tony, Felicity, and Jonathan Dale for taking a risk with me and Mike Morrell and Debbie Gadberry for their editorial input. I also want to thank Winkie Pratney and all those who have endorsed this message. It means so much to me as a new author. Your support has inspired me to believe that this may not be the last book I write.

FOREWORD

by Winkie Pratney

This is a rare and wonderful book. In an age of hype, up-marketed ministry and talk-show host dearth of content, Paul has given us a genuine gem rooted in something I believe is very close to God's heart.

Approach *Jesus Has Left The Building* with all due caution. This is no casual read, no two-dimensional sketch scribbled on some throw-away Mcnapkin on a coffee break. This is *core content* for the coming Church, radical as it gets, a deeply-rooted book of simple conviction palpably born out of a heap of spiritual reality. *You have been warned.* It may indeed disturb, derail perhaps even disenfranchise you, but I promise you it will be well worth it.

In over four decades of working with young people around the Western world, I have never seen a book like this that paints the emerging future in the colors that are coming of revival, restoration and renaissance with such an accurate brush. Paul has done us a great favor in sharing his search, his study and his story.

Jesus Has Left the Building indeed. As for me and my house, we want to be found somewhere out in the highways and byways there with Him. With you and other pilgrims and strangers, we seek those who will risk all to be by His side as He builds that emerging future Kingdom.

Winkie Pratney 2006 A.D.

PROLOGUE

"Don't tell me you can't feel it! Have you ever experienced a greater sense of destiny than you do this very minute?" A friend spoke this to me in his car late one night, traveling down a winding road in southeast Minnesota. We were returning home from a conference in the Twin Cities. He was right. I *had* felt it, and it was unlike anything I have ever known.

I was asked to teach a workshop at this particular Christian conference and was given the last scheduled slot of the weekend. By this time, those in attendance were certainly weary from all the activity of the last few days. Only about twenty people came to my session called *Church in the Year 2027.* I had doubts that the topic of my workshop could compete with the themes going on in the rooms on either side of us. From one end, the worship music workshop sent the sound of horns and cymbals permeating the walls of our room. On the other side, we could hear men shouting; this was a workshop designed to teach believers how to prophesy. I felt God showing me something prophetic through this experience. Other more popular themes in the church seemed to be drowning out what I had to say. At the time, the church at large didn't seem ready for this message.

Despite the noise, I was amazed at how those in my class were able to keep with me. In fact, one man fell to his knees right in front of me while I was teaching, and began to weep and repent. This had never happened to me before. God's presence in the room was very strong, and although this small group represented a minority of the believers attending the conference, God was confirming the truth and relevancy of this topic to us, which has now become the very message of this book.

That night in the car my friend recalled many of the things he heard me say in the workshop. He was so excited. He told me I should write a book. This was it, the moment of destiny. I could hardly contain the overwhelming sense of urgency that I felt to write this book. I instantly understood that this was something I had to do. It was a divine mandate. This happened over four years ago and what you are about to embark upon was birthed that night.

Jesus Has Left the Building is a story about me, the generation that I belong to, and where I believe Jesus is taking the church. The first half of this book describes how God has uniquely prepared a global youth culture to take the expression of Christianity in the West to a whole new level. Actually, this book is not proclaiming anything new at all. It is a vision of what has been and what will be again. It examines what God has done in the past in order to understand what He is doing now. We must look back to be able to move forward. The second half of the book uncovers some of the secrets and lessons we can learn from the church that Jesus started.

This book does not waste effort criticizing the church. My purpose is not to attack the organized church. I do not wish to add further division or controversy to the body of Christ. It would be prideful to do so and very grievous to the Spirit of God. This book reflects my personal and very painful journey away from institutional Christianity. What has driven my quest for a new experience with "church" has been a growing internal dissatisfaction with the alarming contrast between what I read in the gospels and the Christianity that I have known. This book presents you with a vision of "church according to Jesus," which will most likely cast a shadow on any experience that falls short of it.

This is not a book about house churches. In fact, it goes beyond the idea of taking "church" and pouring it into a home. We are not going to concern ourselves with preaching a successful or correct form and model of church. Instead, this book presents the real possibility of leaving behind "church" (as we know it) altogether, to experience an authentic expression of Christ out in the real world.

This is also not another book about how to reach and minister to postmodern people. Although I will briefly explain some of the pertinent aspects of postmodernism, it will be only to bring understanding of how God is using culture to set the stage for what He is about to do. This is a prophetic book in that it looks at our times from God's perspective, comparing them to how He has worked in previous periods of history, specifically biblical history.

My hope is that *Jesus Has Left the Building* will bring clarity to both those who are still within formalized structures of worship and those who are on a spiritual journey outside organized religion. My desire is that you will see the hand of God preparing His people for the greatest revelation of God's glory the earth has ever known. God is repositioning His representatives to be close by, to show and tell the person of Jesus to the many who will yet believe the gospel. And you, following Jesus' lead, can take one large step towards that end. Jesus has left the building. Don't you want to see where He's going?

CHAPTER ONE

Outside The Walls

"Your ministry must die!" I remember those words like it was yesterday, and yet they were spoken to me well over a decade ago. At the time, there was probably nothing more horrible that could have been said to me. After almost five years, something so precious was coming to an end. I was perplexed. To be honest, I cried like a baby. This was my baby! How could God be telling me that I had to let it go?

COME TO THE CROSS

It all started back at a Christian family camp when I was fifteen years old. Under a beautiful night sky, I asked God to take my life and use me in any way He wanted to. The only way I can explain what happened to me in that moment was that God lifted me into His loving face, speaking these words: "Paul, I need you." I know that this doesn't make any sense theologically. God doesn't need anything. He is perfectly complete in Himself. And yet, Father graciously spoke to this young teenager to enlist me into His purposes. I accepted.

The next evening, after my church's worship service, I took my guitar and my friends together down to the beach to worship God. We did this night after night for eleven days, crying, laughing, praying, bowing and dancing on the sand. A fire was ignited in our hearts. If I'd only known how deep this flame would burn.

The fire came home with us. What happened at camp did not stay there like a buried treasure. When we returned to Winnipeg, our hometown, I asked these new young comrades of mine to come over to my parents' house to pray and worship together. We would gather officially once a month and unofficially all the time. We loved to be together with Jesus. It started with ten of us, but after only a few months we had fifty youth cramming into the basement of the house. We knew that God had lit a fire, and it was going to spread.

One afternoon a few of us came together to talk about the direction we were to take. We felt God was calling us to move from my house into something more public. We decided to start a ministry called Come to the Cross where we would hold monthly youth meetings focusing on praise and worship, preaching Jesus, and delivering young people from oppression through the power of prayer.

We held our first public meeting at a church facility in September of 1988 and over 100 youth stormed our doors. The momentum continued each month and one year later we had over 700 teens coming every month to our gatherings. The meetings would last for more than four hours. We would sing and dance like King David. I often think back to those times. Hundreds of youth didn't come to listen to a tight band, watch a smooth running operation, or be entertained with a high gloss, semi-professional presentation of religion. It was raw. It was real. It was passionate and the teachers were their peers. The worship team, the preachers and the ministry team were all under the age of twenty.

Some of the older leaders in the churches around us asked how God could use untrained youth for such a significant ministry responsibility. The religious elite in the fourth chapter of Acts followed the same line of questioning when a few uneducated fishermen started turning Jerusalem upside down with the kingdom of God. I'd have to say that in most ways I was a better leader when I was seventeen years old, operating by dependency on the Holy Spirit and not by the "tricks" I would later learn in ministry training. Tragically, you can learn to study without revelation, preach without anointing, and lead with words but not by example. Ministry itself became sour to me, and I came to a place where I had to repent for depending on myself. I have now come back to where I started—dependency on Jesus.

But in those days, since we didn't know what we were doing, we desperately needed the help of the Holy Spirit. On the mornings of our rallies we would arrive at the building at 10 a.m. to set up the sound equipment. We would have a short music practice, order a bucket of chicken, and break for lunch. This was our ritual. After lunch we would retreat into a small, dark room in the basement of the building and lie there waiting on God until the meeting started. We would wait for His voice for five to six hours, sometimes praying and sometimes sleeping, but mostly praying. We'd get instruction from God on everything that was supposed to happen that night. Our sensitivity to God's presence was sharpened in that room, so that we could follow any slight changes in the blowing of the Spirit's wind. God was always faithful to show us the way. Isn't that what God prefers?

One of the outcomes of these extended times of waiting on God was the release of miracles and healing. One particular night before our Come to the Cross meeting, God spoke to me that someone was coming to the meeting who was deaf. God wanted to heal that person and showed me that He would indicate the precise time in the evening that this was to happen.

During the singing, I kept asking the Lord for the moment of healing but no answer came. When it was time to announce some of the upcoming events, I heard "Now!" from the Holy Spirit. My mind briefly rejected the timing of it (the announcements are so "un-spiritual!"), but since it's futile to argue with Someone who is always right, I stopped in mid-sentence and asked if anyone in the room had brought a deaf person with them.

Out of hundreds of youth there was one person who was fully deaf in one ear. He came forward before the crowd, and we performed little tests to determine what he could hear before I prayed. After I prayed, we did the tests again and saw that God healed him. The whole place exploded with praise and faith. The next thing I knew people were lining up to be healed. God did many miracles that night. There were individuals who had come into the meeting on crutches and by the end of the evening, were running around the room unaided. The tears flowed, hearts were encouraged and God was glorified. It was a holy moment.

"I WANT TO DO THIS STUFF OUTSIDE THE WALLS"

For much of my teenage life I experienced a localized revival. We had seen thousands of young people come through our doors. Many of them became followers of Jesus through our ministry. We saw dozens of miracles and hundreds of teenagers spiritually revitalized. This momentum showed no sign of waning. I had great plans for this ministry. We were hoping to plant churches around the world, and I thought I would be working with these people for the rest of my life. There was nothing on earth more important to me, so when I heard God tell me to end it I couldn't understand why. I sobbed and grieved over this. I told

Father that I truly needed Him to confirm it by speaking to the others on our team.

Soon after, we had a team meeting and one by one each member began to share how they felt that Come to the Cross was supposed to end. There was no obvious indication that things were winding down. In fact, we saw more fruit and maturation in our ministry the last year we operated than ever before. I did not understand it, but I knew what God was saying. So, we obeyed Him and held our final meeting in September of 1992.

We went out with a bang. We celebrated all that the Lord had done in the five years of this spiritual youth revival. There was an excitement in the air, as well as a sadness that something so wonderful to so many of us was coming to a close.

I preached a message that night that was more relevant than I realized at the time. I felt that God had given me a small glimpse into why He was ending this ministry. He truly was moving among us but most of it was contained behind the four walls of a church building. This is the declaration that came from my mouth that night, our last night: "God wants to take this stuff and do it *outside the walls.*" God's heart was to bring His glory into plain view, into the real world. Jesus was leaving the building.

To be honest with you, I had no idea what God meant by this statement "outside the walls." God wanted Come to the Cross to die because He was going to do something new for us. Somehow I knew that if we were to continue the way we were going, we would not only miss this new thing, but perhaps even resist it. When I woke up Monday morning that next week, I said to the Lord, "I'm ready for it—bring it on!" I had no clue what this fresh move of God was about, nor did I expect that the next ten years of my life would be filled with pain, disillusionment, and obscurity. He was preparing me.

A PASTOR WHO HATES GOING TO CHURCH

After Come to the Cross, I threw myself into serving at my local congregation. I was a young man full of vision and excitement for what I could do in the church. I quickly "moved up the ladder" of ministry and caught the attention of leadership. It wasn't very long before I was hired for youth work and evangelism. Here I was in my early twenties, now on staff at a large, "successful" church. I sat with the elders at the very top level of church government, learning and being groomed for leadership. However, something started dying in me. I began to ask *the question.*

Do you know the question? It is the question that drives innovation. It is the question of reformation. It's what Martin Luther asked that fateful day as he was crawling up the stone stairs of the cathedral, paying penance for his sins. With bloody knees, he asked himself, "Why?" "Why am I doing this?" "Why are we doing this?" Children ask instinctively what many adults have stopped asking. They are always learning, adapting, changing while we are lulled into a deep sleep of passivity and stagnancy. Perhaps it is because of this question that you are now reading this book.

I began to experience distaste for organized "Christianity." I found myself asking *why* incessantly. Why were we giving more time to the building project, when the marriages of our leaders were falling apart? Why was our staff cutting their salaries to pay for the ever growing financial needs of our building? Why did we spend so much time trying

to figure out how to organize the church, when there were people hurt-
ing and lost, right across the street? Why did we spend thousands of
dollars and hours doing evangelistic outreach, seeing little to no fruit?
Why did everyone have to talk and look the same to be accepted? Why
were we all so lonely, even though we saw each other at church meetings
three or four times a week?

An opportunity was presented to me to become the pastor of a small
church, just outside the city. I desperately needed something new. My
view of ministry in the church needed major resuscitation. I accepted
the position, naively thinking that at least as the "pastor," I could avoid
falling into some of the pitfalls I had experienced in the previous church.
I was mistaken. I didn't know it at the time, but God was leading me
into disillusionment, where I'd long for something different. He was
positioning me to be right where I needed to be.

The question continued to haunt me, and I asked myself "Why?"
every Sunday morning as I drove to "church." For a whole year the
depression would hit me each Saturday night, as I anticipated the church
service the next day. What was happening to me? My belief in what I
was doing was diminishing.

I guess I was feeling many different things at the time. As the
"pastor" I was under a tremendous pressure to make things happen.
I hated the feeling that I was a performer. No matter how much I
preached about all believers being ministers, I was fighting against hundreds of years of tradition that said otherwise. It was bigger than me.
I also felt that the people I was leading didn't need any more "feeding."
There comes a time when believers should mature to a point where they
are able to feed themselves and others in need. We know so much today.
Why are so many Christians staying in infancy? I also came to the real-

ization that I was lonely behind the walls of the church, and had no friends outside those walls. What I was doing was completely irrelevant to the people in our culture, especially to the emerging generations.

Do you know what I'm talking about? Don't you feel like there is something wrong? Our culture seems to have a problem with "institutional religion." Do they see something we are not seeing?

ORGANIC?

I would like to give you a primitive definition of what I mean by "organic" church. I say *primitive* because the rest of the book will complete the picture. You might want to look up the word *organic* in the dictionary. If you do, you will discover that this word describes things that relate or belong to the class of chemical compounds that have a carbon base, and only living things have a carbon base. Therefore, organic is the word for *life*, right down to the chemical construction. If it's organic, it is alive or the product of something that's alive. The church is a living, breathing entity. It is the body of Jesus.

Organic can also refer to something being clean of any synthetic chemicals or injected additives. This is what we mean when we say *organic food*. It is clean, simple, healthy, and close to nature. Unfortunately, many of our churches cannot be described this way. They have been injected with synthetic material, man-made toxic compounds of the carnal nature.

What we traditionally call "church" is often two entities, a blend of mechanical and biological elements held together by a form of fusion. There are two churches, the institutional church and the organic church. The picture I see is a living plant intertwined with a lifeless silk plant.

The silk plant looks real, but it is not alive and doesn't produce fruit. It is the inorganic, fake plant that is falsely called the church. It may be an organization of the church, but not the church itself. The question arises, "Is this organization perfectly suited to fulfill the basic mandate of Christ's ministry on earth?" All too often we see that the mechanical parts inevitably only restrict and repress the genuine life of the organic members.

In my experience, I loved being with God's people. But there was something else interfering with our relationships and life together. This subtle, but very powerful system of values and practices does not seem to have its root in Jesus. I often use the following words synonymously (sometimes humorously), to describe this hindrance: institutional church, organized church, the religious system, the system, the corporate machine, the monster, the building, the matrix. Periodically, I will make statements that question the legitimacy of "church." When this happens, please know that I am not referring to the true church, made up of all believers in Christ, but to the organization typically called "church."

So, how would I define "the building"? What is it exactly that Jesus is supposedly walking away from? Well, you might be dealing with an institutional understanding if you maintain or accept the following ideas about "church:"

- it's somewhere you go
- it happens on a special day of the week
- you have a professional to tell you what to do
- all it requires of you is attendance and fees paid
- there exists a hierarchical command structure
- meetings come before people

- it has committees
- it has programs
- it has a corporate vision
- it has a corporate name
- it segregates itself from other believers
- it is more concerned with structure than content
- quality is sacrificed for quantity

I risk being quite easily misunderstood. You may think that I am against structure. This is not what I'm trying to communicate. Structure is a characteristic of life itself. To remove structure is to bypass productivity altogether. Our bodies wouldn't be able to do anything if it were not for the delicate balance of our skeletal and muscular systems. We would literally be a blob on the floor, not capable of activity necessary in keeping us alive. However, are the structures we customarily call "church" appropriately designated? Church as we know it today looks extremely different from what it was in the beginning. But things are changing.

Structure will change only because that which needs to be contained is something brand new. Whenever you have new wine, as Jesus put it, you must put it into a new wineskin. Christianity, as we know it, is morphing and its appearance will be a reality that most of us haven't seen in a long time, perhaps two thousand years.

Now I probably really have your attention. Trust me, if you continue with me on this ride, you won't believe where we're going. Jesus is the one leading the way.

CHAPTER TWO

NEW WINE NEEDS A NEW WINESKIN

"Pregnant women shouldn't drink wine." This wasn't actually too difficult for my wife Tamara since she'd never been an excessive drinker. We had done this before, and the new baby was due April 22, 2000. There was a slight interruption in the plan though. April 22 had come and gone, and my wife's tummy was still quite popped. Big brother Jordan, who was two years old, came on his due date. What was this new kid's problem?

Months before, when we first discovered that Tamara was expecting, the Lord showed me that He wanted to speak to me through the birth of this child. I had been looking forward to this moment. I would meet the long anticipated baby, and hear God speak to me. However, the delay was certainly taxing.

We waited a few days, which soon turned into a week. When was this going to happen? I remember feeling like we couldn't make any plans. This baby could come at any moment. We just waited and waited. Finally, on the tenth day Tamara went into labor and within an hour our son Benjamin was born.

This was a shock to me. I was sure that we were having a girl. When I saw that my little "girl" came out with some extra equipment, I yelled out, "Tam, it's a boy!" We wept with joy. The baby didn't come how I'd expected, but when I laid eyes on my son, it didn't matter. I fell instantly in love with him.

Later, when we got home from the hospital, I remembered that the Lord wanted to speak to me out of this experience. God led me to Luke 2:7, which says, "And she brought forth her firstborn Son, and wrapped Him in swaddling cloths, and laid Him in a manger, because there was no room for them in the inn." The Holy Spirit showed me that the child represented the new thing that God wanted to do. He reminded me about all the prophetic words that I had heard in the past; promises of an outpouring of His Spirit in the emerging generation and a fresh expression of Christ in our Western culture.

There were two things I learned from the birth of my son. First, what came wasn't what I expected. I thought he was a *she*, but she was actually a *he*. Second, I had to wait for it. The Lord was showing me that what is coming is not going to be what people expect, and only those who are willing to wait will be able to receive it. I waited ten days for Benjamin. Similarly, the early church waited ten days in the upper room to receive the Holy Spirit on the day of Pentecost.

The King of Glory did not enter this world as we might have expected. The night he was born, the world went on with business-as-usual. The only people, other than Jesus' family, that even really knew He had come were some lowly shepherds, occultists from the east, and elderly Simeon and Anna. The latter two had been waiting to see the salvation of Israel all their lives. They saw Him.

What about His accommodations? The Son of God wasn't born in a palace or even a four star hotel. When I read Luke 2:7, after the birth of my son, it was this phrase that hit me: "There was no room for Him in the inn." This is the Messiah, the savior of the world. Here He lies in a feeding trough for animals. What a dirty and messy place to have a baby.

The ancient and original version of Christianity that I believe is returning is not going to happen in the place that you would expect. There is no room for this in the clean and controlled environment of institutional church. It's going to happen out in the manger, in that dirty place, where the poor and the seekers will find Him. It's going to happen outside the building.

A PARADIGM SHIFT

I've just recently begun to comprehend an important aspect of understanding revelation from God. Receiving the message is only half the equation. The minute that the words hit the "grid" in our brain, the moment we perceive it with our intellect, those words get corrupted. God's thoughts are not our thoughts, and His ways are so much different than ours. We think we know what God means, but "message sent is not message received." We not only need God to communicate the message to us, we need God to help us understand it. We need Him working on both ends.

This "mind grid" that we have is our world view, and it has been constructed by our personal history and experiences. It is our paradigm. A paradigm is like a map. If I had a map of L.A. but I was actually in New York, nothing on the map would correspond with what I'm experiencing in reality. Whenever we go to a new place, we need a new map.

Jesus put it this way: "You can't put new wine into an old wineskin." When God speaks to us about the future, the container is as important as the content. There needs to be a new container for the new wine He desires to give us. The last ten years of my life has been about deconstructing the grid (or the paradigm) I had about church. God is revealing a new container for the new things He is going to do. This new wineskin is for a wine that will be poured outside the walls.

There are many times in Scripture where God destroys human grids to make room for the moving of His Spirit. There are also just as many examples of people who harden their hearts to God's process of change and miss the hour of their visitation. One perfect example of this is found early in Jesus' ministry, in His hometown of Nazareth. Jesus had just returned from forty days in the wilderness, and He joined with others from His community at the synagogue. As He must have done many times in His life, Jesus stood up to read Scripture. He read one of the most quoted prophetic Messianic passages from Isaiah 61. Those who were listening to the reading that day would have automatically recognized it. It was something they would have memorized, and assumed to understand. Basically, this was their hope of the justice that would come one glorious day. The Messiah would bring His people liberation. As Jesus went on to explain what the passage meant, all who heard marveled at His words. They said to one another, "Isn't this Joseph and Mary's boy?" They were truly impressed at how gracious His words were. Where did the boy learn so much? They were pleased by what Jesus was saying, until He hit a nerve.

This is the place where the people got so angry at Jesus that they literally pushed Him out of the synagogue, out of the city and to the edge of a cliff in order to throw Him off. These were the people Jesus grew up with. We are talking about uncles and aunts, school mates, and friends of the family. Just imagine having one of the children in your church community that you witnessed growing up, speaking in the congregation one day as a young woman. Can you think of anything she could possibly say that would stir enough turbulent commotion to cause friends and family to want to kill that child? What did Jesus say that could incite such a level of rage?

The members of the synagogue that day thought they knew how Isaiah 61 was going to play out. They were hoping in the Messiah and they believed that He would come for them, as Jews. Every man that entered that place with Jesus would have recited this short prayer: "I thank you, God, that I am not a woman, a leper, or a Gentile." What fueled the rage was not that Jesus inferred that He was the fulfillment of the prophecy. What really made them angry was when Jesus described who it was that the Messiah was coming for.

> But I tell you truly, many widows were in Israel in the days of Elijah, when the heaven was shut up three years and six months, and there was a great famine throughout all the land; but to none of them was Elijah sent except to Zarephath, in the region of Sidon, to a woman who was a widow. And many lepers were in Israel in the time of Elisha the prophet, and none of them was cleansed except Naaman the Syrian. So all those in the synagogue, when they heard these things, were filled with wrath. (Luke 4:25-28)

Jesus is comparing Himself to Elijah and Elisha. Whom did these prophets minister to? It is these same kinds of people that the Messiah will set free and heal. He speaks of a woman (widow) and a leper, who were both Gentiles. Jesus was telling His home "church" that He indeed was the Messiah, and that He was here to preach good news to the poor, especially women, lepers, and Gentiles.

This is why they got so angry. Jesus was touching their prejudice.

He was showing them that God had something different in mind than what they originally thought. God was coming to visit them in a way that they didn't expect. Not only did they not expect it, they rejected the whole notion of who Jesus had come for. These people knew the prophetic Scriptures and yet when it began to happen before them, they could not see it. They needed a new map. Their way of thinking was hostile to the ways of God. We too must be careful that we do not get offended with who Jesus befriends or what He is doing outside of our little box.

We can see another example of this in the life of Peter. In Matthew 16, Peter received a revelation of who Jesus is. He declared with faith and conviction, "You are the Christ, the Son of the living God." Jesus affirmed Peter and showed him that he didn't receive this from any person, but that God Himself opened up Peter's eyes to see. Wow! Peter had a word from God. He had a divine revelation of Jesus. However, Peter had an old grid that needed some demolition.

In the very next passage, Jesus told His disciples that He was going to be killed and would rise on the third day. At this point, Peter actually rebuked Jesus. "Jesus, you have it all wrong. The Messiah is not supposed to die." (Paraphrased) You see, Peter knew that Jesus was the Messiah by a revelation from God, but that was only one side of the coin. Peter's grid or understanding of what the Messiah was and what He would do was faulty. Jesus responded to Peter by saying, "Get behind me Satan, for you are not thinking the thoughts of God but the thoughts of men." Jesus saw that the root of human thinking was satanic. We have to assume that our thoughts, apart from divine intervention, are wrong. Not only do we need to hear from God, we also need God to destroy our faulty thinking and give us new heavenly paradigms.

Peter needed his grid changed. When he was rebuked by the Lord, I believe he went away very hurt, thinking, "What did I say that was so wrong?" From that moment on, we read about how Jesus changed His focus as He faced the reality of the cross. The disciples were quickly disappointed and discouraged, as the crowds of followers turned away at Jesus' hard words.

Jesus seemed to have intentionally made it impossible for people to follow Him. After the crowds were gone, all that was left were His twelve. At one point, Jesus even asked them, "Are you going to leave me too?" Ultimately, they all did forsake Him on the night He was betrayed. This did not look like the glorious Messiah king that they were anticipating. Peter was so discouraged and confused that he even denied the Lord. Yet he thought he could die for Jesus. Peter didn't even know his own heart. Failure was painful, but it was the necessary wilderness that would ultimately give Peter the true understanding of Christ's love and forgiveness. By falling and being restored, Peter came to understand the other side of the equation. He was given a new map. He now knew why the Messiah would have to die, and he had a story to tell.

I think many of us have been placed in a wilderness in order to reformat the way we think. God is helping change our perception. There's a preparation going on for what the future church is going to look like. However, it's a preparation of death. Peter came face to face with the fear of death, and failed in it. That was Peter's process and mine as well. Remember, the Lord spoke through me at the last Come to the Cross meeting that he was going to take this stuff and do it outside the walls. I've been in a process of years of dying, failing, and living in obscurity. In this place I have learned that God loves me and that is why I am already successful. It is here in the wilderness that I have fallen in love again with the Bridegroom, whom I'd honestly rather be writing about. Christ is preeminent.

Talking about the church has been necessary and I'm willing to do it because old paradigms are fading away, and we are relearning what the container needs to be for the coming move of God's Spirit. However, I hope I don't talk about the "new wineskin" for the rest of my life. If that is the case, something is horribly wrong. This is really not about the wineskin; it's all about the new wine. I'm starting to thirst more and more for this new wine. Having a container with nothing in it is very unsatisfying. I don't want to talk about the church anymore; I want to live in the life of the Holy Spirit.

Having said all this, my burden here is primarily about the container or the wineskin that will be able to hold the new wine. I pray that God uses this writing to deconstruct faulty grids in your thinking, as He's doing for me. Improper ways of thinking regarding the church will most definitely emerge as we travel through these pages together. You may be going through the unpleasant but necessary process of a paradigm shift. Allow yourself to make room for God to alter what you've always thought. We don't want to miss the baby in the manger while sitting in the hot tub over at the Holiday Inn.

A TOKEN OF THINGS TO COME

It was May of 1998, during a time of prayer. The Holy Spirit informed me that there would be a girl named Cherry that would call and that she was going to ask me to help her with her friends. I was shown this ahead of time, in order to place significance on this event. This would soon be an important moment in my journey.

I actually had met Cherry once before. Her parents belonged to the church that I was leading, and she had come with them one Easter Sunday morning. Earlier that week, her parents informed me that she was coming to church. I noticed how much they were concerned for her. She was living in the city and going to university at the time. She hadn't been in church for quite a while. That Sunday was the only time I had ever met her. Why was God telling me that she would call me? Well, I really thought I would receive a call from her that week, but it didn't come.

A month later, my growing dissatisfaction at the church came to a head. My heart was just not there. Everything inside me was saying, "Leave the building!" I resigned at the end of June. Soon after, I preached my last Sunday in that church and I was done. The day I left they held a picnic for me, gave me a card and a $50 gift certificate to a Christian bookstore. I received a pat on the back, and away I went.

The next morning, I was lying in bed wondering what I was going to do now. I had no job, no income, and no idea what to do with my life. Later that afternoon, guess who called me? It was Cherry. I suddenly remembered the word God gave me over a month before. She went on to explain how one of her friends was exhibiting what she believed to be demonic manifestations. She didn't know who to call. The only name running through her head was mine. She said to me, "I thought maybe you could help."

I asked my father to come with me, and the two of us met with her and some of her friends that night. Before praying with this young man, we explained where demons came from and how Jesus had all the authority. We spent most of the evening talking about Jesus. It was amazing. Most of them had some kind of connection to Christianity in the past, but didn't really know what Jesus was all about. We did pray for the guy, as well as all the others. Each one was deeply touched by the Spirit of God. It was an incredible time of ministry that continued for over four hours.

As I drove home that night, my spirit was on fire. I thought to myself, "This sure beats running a church." Suddenly, I remembered the last message I preached at Come to the Cross. God wanted to do the stuff "outside the walls." Then it dawned on me. Everything that happened that night either happened in the coffee shop, or back at a house, or out on the street. Jesus was touching people who would never set foot in a "church," and He was doing it all in the world that they lived in. Jesus had left the building.

Before going to bed that night, God showed me that this was a "token." It was a glimpse into the future. It was just enough to whet my appetite, keep me interested and searching for something that I believe is going to be commonplace. This night was a taste of things to come.

THE SPACE BETWEEN OLD AND NEW

Matthew 9:14-17 is the passage where Jesus uses the "wineskin" metaphor. Some of John's disciples asked Jesus, "Why do we and the Pharisees fast often, but your disciples do not fast?" I'm sure they thought to themselves, "Everybody knows that fasting is a non-negotiable." These guys had tons of Bible verses to support the fact that anyone serious about God should fast.

I find it odd that John the Baptist still had followers at that point. Why didn't those disciples of John make the shift over to Jesus? John told them to follow Jesus. John the Baptist said that he wasn't worthy enough to untie Jesus' shoes. He also proclaimed that he must decrease and Christ must increase. It seems like some people that were in with the last move of God, represented by John, couldn't make the shift into the new move of God.

It is in this passage that Jesus talks about the fact that you can't put new wine into an old wineskin. If you do that, the new wine that is still fermenting will destroy the old wineskin. You need to make a new container for it. The fasting that the Pharisees and disciples of John did was an old wineskin. They fasted to mourn and to grieve over sin. Jesus said that while He was with them, there would be no mourning. But when Jesus leaves them one day, they will fast.

The new wine of Jesus and His new covenant couldn't be poured into the wineskin of the old covenant. Fasting had to change if it was going to be able to be used in the new covenant. The old forms of Judaism would not be able to contain the fresh forms of the gospel. Grace could not be poured into a system of legalism. The disciples did fast in Acts, but not to mourn sin. Fasting changed its container for the new thing. Fasting in the new covenant is a response of faith to the leading of the Holy Spirit. They fasted in the book of Acts to wait on God and hear His voice. They fasted for release into new anointing and ministry. The wineskin of fasting was new.

The key to this is the space between the old wineskin and the new. While Jesus was with His disciples for three years, they literally stopped engaging in many of their older ways. The religious people around them, steeped in tradition, were constantly criticizing them for not keeping the rules. Some of these activities were even "biblical" and as important as fasting.

I believe the disciples were "detoxing." The period of time between leaving behind the old and walking in the new is a time of withdrawal. When we have engaged in activity for a long time, it is hard not to fall into certain ruts. If structure needs to change, there needs to be a period of time that you abstain from that structure. It's just like getting off drugs.

Karl Marx was not far from the truth when he said, "Religion is the opiate of the masses." There is a certain "fix" that we get from our religious rituals. It does feel like a form of withdrawal when we refrain from these activities. I am convinced there must be special seasons of intimacy with Jesus, getting all the old ways out of our system.

This is what it was like for me for a long while after I resigned from my pastoral position. Tamara and I stopped "going to church." Instead, we invited believing friends over to the house for fellowship. We joined in a journey together with four other families, just to be with Jesus, and to detoxify. I questioned everything I once did. There were no "sacred cows." I have to admit, we threw out the baby with the bath water on a few occasions. However, the Lord's leadership was strong and He was gracious to give the "baby" back to us.

We were in a process of rediscovery. I wanted to know the reason for everything we did and that it was the heart of God and not just tradition. I sought God for revelation as to how He wants things done in the days we live in. For many months our gatherings consisted of conversations over a cup of coffee, and we learned how to be relational again. What we were doing didn't look right to those with a religious spirit, but we were experiencing new freedom and life in Jesus.

"YOU ARE JUST REACTING"

People at times may feel that someone with a message like this one is only reacting to the painful experiences with the church in their own lives. I know that individuals have thought this about me. Even some of my friends and family don't quite understand why I'm not "going to church." They still believe that I am hurt in some way, or that it was because I was burned by the politics within church leadership. I freely admit that in the beginning it was a reaction. If you put your hand on a hot stove, it is a very natural and instant reflex to pull away. The role of reaction is useful if you are in immediate danger. Reaction is also a very necessary part of adaptation, which is a characteristic of living things. We learn from pain and we adjust ourselves accordingly. There would be no change or growth if we didn't respond to our environment. However, once appropriate changes have been made there is no need to keep the wound open.

A negative reaction to a bad experience with church is understandable for a short season, but can be fatal if resentment is coddled. You cannot stay in that place of hurt and anger. It will destroy you and spread to others like a contagious disease. Bono, front man of the band U2, wrote in their song *Peace on Earth*, "They say what you mock will surely overtake you, and you become a monster so the monster doesn't break you." If you hold on to bitterness, your heart hardens and you become the very thing you hate. There comes a point when one has to let it all go and forgive. A friend once told me that "unforgiveness is like drinking poison, but expecting the other person to die." Truly there are too many individuals consumed with anger towards the institutional church. This kind of attitude is not helping anyone, especially those who have it.

I'm also equally misunderstood by people thinking that I just don't like structure. The organization of the church is only a peripheral issue. The real problem lies beneath. It is an evil that exists in the depths of humanity itself and no one is outside its grasp. I am not attacking externals like "Sunday services," "pastors," "church budgets," "Sunday school," "church buildings," "mega-churches," or anything to do with size or how congregations typically organize themselves.

Also, I am certainly not preaching that house churches are *the* answer, and that all other forms are unbiblical. It goes much deeper than this. I'm referring to a way of thinking about church that is rooted in carnality and the worst of human tradition. You can still have these in house churches. Changing the structure in and of itself is not the magic cure. If you still think in an old way, meeting in homes is worse than going to church on Sunday. At least in "church" there is a crowd and some live music to keep you awake. Meeting in a house yet still having a "bricks and mortar" mentality is the worst of both worlds.

I learned this the hard way. Years after leaving institutional forms of church I still found that the system was inside of me. The very things I hated lurked within. Getting out of the "organized church" was only half the battle. Getting the "organization" out of me has been nearly impossible to do. This was much the case with the Hebrew slaves that were delivered under the ministry of Moses in Egypt. By the hand of God, Moses was able to lead the people out of Egypt, but was helpless to extract Egypt out of the people. Egypt was more than a place with roads and buildings; it was a system that permeated the hearts of those who had grown up within its walls. I found that even though I was out, the ideas that were engraved upon my mind by religion were very difficult to undo. Fortunately, being free is more than just a possibility. Paul, the apostle, is a perfect example of a man who was once bound by religiosity, but found release by knowing God's grace.

I too feel liberated. It is truly wonderful. The voices in my head have been silenced. They once ruled my mind, telling me that nothing was ever right. I no longer see others as a means to attaining my secret ambitions. I've learned just to love without strings attached. There is no one to please. I don't really care about what others think of me. I don't care if I succeed or fail. It doesn't change how God feels about me. I don't need to control others and others don't have a hold on me. I don't need to perform to be accepted. I can be who I am and be loved as I am. I'm not expecting someone else to draw me into God. I know Him for myself and I tell others around me that they can know Him directly as well. I don't feel guilty anymore. I trust Jesus' leadership in my life even more than I trust myself. He is making me what I always wanted to be. I can rest. I am free.

CHAPTER THREE

THE APOSTOLIC DREAM

It was a sunny and beautiful spring afternoon. I had no idea how important that day would be for me. I decided to spend the afternoon in prayer. As I was praying the Lord spoke several critical things to me. One of those things came in the form of a vision.

I saw a book cover in my mind's eye. As the picture focused in on the cover, the title read *The Apostolic Dream*. The subtitle of the book was, *That the World Would See Jesus in the Face of His People*. I was intrigued by this statement. The Lord spoke to my heart and inspired me to search this message out in the Scriptures. As a result, this has become my life message and passion. Let me introduce you to the apostolic dream.

ALL THE EARTH SHALL BE FILLED

The people of Israel saw some pretty amazing things. They were delivered from slavery to Egypt by ten plagues, sovereign acts of God's awesome power. They had seen the sea open up before their eyes, and watched the same waters crush the strength of their enemies. Moses led them to the holy mountain where they received the Law. Early in their journey of freedom, they revealed their fickle and unbelieving hearts. At one point when Moses delayed in his return from the top of the mountain, they fashioned for themselves a golden calf to worship. All the while, the Lord spoke to Moses as "a man speaks to his friend." (Exodus 33:11)

I find it amazing that God considered Moses His friend. I know we all like the idea of God being our friend. Who wouldn't want the most powerful person in the universe to be your close acquaintance? However, it's a different thing when God calls a person His friend. A friend is someone you can totally be yourself with. What you see is what you get. You can share your heart without fear of being judged or misunderstood. You can be completely transparent with a true friend.

The story that I'm about to tell you, found in Numbers 14:11-21, is all about how God opened up His heart to His friend, Moses. It's here in these pages of Scripture that we get a glimpse of God's passion and His dream for planet earth.

God was upset. He had led His people right to the edge of the wilderness, at the very entry point into the land He had promised to them. The people sent in twelve spies to see if the land was everything God said it was. As you know, ten of them came back saying, "The land is incredible alright, but we'll never see it. The people there are gigantic, their cities are well defended, and we're like little tiny bugs compared to them." (my paraphrase)

The people heard their report and their hearts sank with unbelief. There was no way any of them were going into the Promised Land. God was angry and He needed to talk to someone about it. He needed His friend. The Lord said to Moses, "How long will these people reject Me?" I could just picture God sighing as He said that. Moses probably had a hard time hearing God tell him this. Things got even more intense after God declared, "I will strike them with pestilence and disinherit them, and I will make of you a nation greater and mightier than they."

I don't know about you, but that would have been a tempting offer to me. "You mean I could be the main man? I could be the father of the nation?" But this was more than a test for Moses. I believe God had something for him to discover. He wanted Moses to come to some conclusions about God and about what was in God's heart.

We do this with our kids. I remember playing with my son Jordan when he was only two. We were putting the shaped blocks into their proper holes. Sometimes parents pretend they don't know the answer so that their child can figure things out for themselves. I would say, "Hey Jordan, does this square block fit in the round hole?" He probably thought, "Duh...Dad, how old are you?" Of course I knew the answer, but I was attempting to draw the right conclusion out of my son. He would not learn how to reason and think for himself if I always told him the answer.

God at times teaches us this same way. I believe God was making a statement to Moses that initiated a response to search out the truth in the heart of God. I don't believe God wanted to wipe His people out. He only presented the idea to His friend to reveal a greater purpose in having brought His people this far.

Moses began to think it out loud. "If God killed all these people, then Egypt and all the nations of the earth would hear about it, and God's reputation would be on the line. The nations have heard the reports that the God of Israel is active and alive, and lives with His people. If God would do this thing that He is suggesting, then the nations would say, 'He couldn't do it. He couldn't finish what He started.'" Moses went on to tell God that this is out of character for Him, for He is longsuffering. It takes a lot to get God mad. He doesn't fly off the handle or react thoughtlessly. He also is merciful. Moses asked God to forgive the people. Without hesitation the Lord responded with, "I have pardoned, according to your word."

That didn't take much. It was like God already had forgiven them. So what was this whole exercise about? The next thing God said, in verse 21, reveals what He wanted to show Moses all along. God declared, "As surely as I live, all the earth shall be filled with the glory of the Lord." God was assuring Moses that not only would He not allow His reputation to be distorted before the nations of the earth, but that His plan was to reveal His glory around the world.

The glory of God is what God is made of. It is His character and the substance of who He is. God's plan for this planet is to reveal Himself to every nation and people group on the globe. There is nothing more real than the existence of God. The Bible declares that God exists in the very first verse when it says, "In the beginning God…" God's covenant name Yahweh, given to Moses at the burning bush, means "I am." God is, and there is nothing more certain or true than His existence. And yet there is something that God considers to be as true as He is. God promised us that as "surely as He exists," the whole world will see and know His glory. We can bet our life on the fact that this is the ultimate destiny of planet earth.

God repeats this same statement three times in the Old Testament (Numbers 14:21; Psalm 72:19; Habakkuk 2:14). Repeating something three times is a Hebrew way of putting stronger emphasis on that thought. This happens often throughout the Scriptures, such as when Luke 15 records three parables back-to-back of Jesus describing something that was lost. Another example of this is found on the lips of the angels and living creatures in heaven around the throne who proclaim, "Holy, holy, holy is the Lord." (See Isaiah 6:3 and Revelation 4:8) The host of heaven is revealing that the ultimate expression of God's person is extreme holiness. God is really holy! In this same way, God will certainly and completely permeate the earth with the experiential knowledge of His glory, all of who He is.

INCARNATION

What is more impressive and almost unfathomable is how God is going to accomplish this. If I were God, I would want to take care of this one myself. It's too important to let anyone else mess it up. However, God has something else in mind. He likes to make things harder for Himself, which only appear harder to us because we don't understand that He can do anything. This is what the apostolic dream is all about. God desires to reveal Himself and His glory through us!

I am talking about a very powerful idea called "incarnation." Webster's dictionary defines this word as "made manifest or comprehensible." A synonym of incarnation is the word "embodied." John 1:1 and 1:14 describe something called the *logos*. *Logos* means a transmission of thought, a communication, a word of explanation, an utterance, divine revelation, an oracle. John reveals to us that Jesus is the Logos. He is the divine revelation of God. He is the explanation of who God is. However, this word became "flesh and dwelt among us, and we beheld His glory." The message wasn't communicated from the sky; it took on flesh and blood. The glory of God was covered in skin, and could be seen, heard and touched.

This revelation of the glory of God starts with Jesus, but it goes further. Jesus, on the night He was betrayed, was asked by one of His followers to show them the Father. Jesus responded by saying, "He who has seen Me has seen the Father." (John 14:9) Jesus did the works of the Father and only spoke the words that the Father was speaking. He was the Logos incarnate! The Father could be clearly seen in the face of Jesus. Those around Jesus at the time could see what God was all about. But what about the rest of the world? How would the whole world see the glory of God? Jesus went on to tell His disciples in the same passage that "He who believes in Me, the works that I do he will do also; and greater works than these he will do, because I go to My Father."

Jesus passed the baton. Somehow when this was all set in motion, from the time of Jesus ascending to His place at the right hand of His Father and the sending of the Holy Spirit, believers were to be changed to do the works that Jesus did. As you could see the Father in the face of Jesus, so will the world see Jesus in the face of His followers. God's glory is to be seen in the ones incarnating Jesus.

WHY "APOSTOLIC"?

This is partially why God called it the "apostolic dream." The word *apostolos* is the Greek word that means "sent one." It carries the idea that someone is being sent on the authority of another, to do and say things on the sender's behalf. This delegate is authorized by someone else. Jesus declared, "As the Father has sent Me, I also send you." (John 20: 21) The apostolic dream is a dream in the heart of the Father to have a multitude of "sent ones."

The apostolic ministry is not only about carrying a message. The apostle or "sent one" is the message in bodily form. Apostolic ministry is about representation. When we say or do things in the name of someone else, we are saying that this is the will of the person sending us. When the first apostles healed the sick, they often said, "The Lord heals you." "Even though I'm here, Jesus is doing the healing." When we come in the name of Jesus, we are telling people that Jesus is doing what we are doing or saying what we are saying. We act on His behalf, as representatives or ambassadors of Jesus. This is how the world will see the glory of God. Jesus will be seen in us and through our words and actions.

As the early church spread through the Roman Empire with the gospel, they were known as "followers of the Way." It was in Antioch that the name "Christian" was first used to describe these people. (Acts 11:26) The inhabitants of Antioch must have thought to themselves, "What do we call these extraordinary people?" The word Christian literally means "little Christ." These guys act like Jesus. They are "Jesus people." The citizens of Antioch could see the reflection of Jesus in their faces.

This is the apostolic dream because it is the purpose of God to have an apostolic people. It is a plan to have people from every part of the world, who are sent to represent the person and glory of Jesus. I believe without a doubt that God will fulfill His promise to Moses of His glory covering the earth, by having His people scattered everywhere throughout the world. It's not just sending a satellite signal of a TV preacher to the nations. The world must hear it, see it, and touch it. I believe the glory of God must be in walking distance to every human on the planet. God wants to come close. The truth must be heard and seen, but also handled. (1 John 1:1) People in the world must be loved by Jesus, served by Jesus, hugged by Jesus, have coffee with Jesus; we may be the only Jesus that they see.

This is not only a dream to see an apostolic people emerge, but it is also the dream of the apostles themselves. Although all believers have the potential to be "apostolic," Jesus has given us some equippers called

46

"apostles." These guys are here to empower us to fulfill the dream. Maybe you thought, "Hey wait a minute, aren't apostles dead?" If that were true, this dream would quickly become a nightmare. We need apostles! The truth is, we do indeed have these sent ones among us, and many of them are still hidden, perhaps already outside the walls of the church structure. Let me explain the nature of the apostles we have with us in our present times.

What you may not understand is that there are a few different layers of apostles in the Scriptures. The top level is Jesus. He is the Apostle with a capital "A." (Hebrews 3:1) In the second layer, we have "the twelve apostles of the Lamb." (Revelation 21:14) These are the ones that most people think of when they hear the word "apostle." They are the disciples who followed Christ during His earthly ministry. Jesus specifically appointed twelve of them to be called apostles. They are referred to repeatedly throughout the gospels as the Twelve (e.g. Matthew 10: 2). This is true after Judas Iscariot was replaced by Matthias (Acts 2:14; 6:2; 1 Corinthians 15:5). This numerical designation testifies to their unique position in the economy of God. They all had been eyewitnesses of Christ's ministry from the baptism of John to His resurrection (Acts 1:21-26). They are pictured as having the foundational ministry of confirming the words that the Old Testament prophets spoke concerning the coming Messiah. This is a closed number. There are no more "apostles of the Lamb."

There is a third layer of apostolic ministry that exists to this very day. The New Testament makes a number of references to the ministry gift of "apostle," given by the risen Christ to His church, for her continual edification until He returns (Ephesians 4:11-13; 1 Corinthians 12: 28). Indeed, a number of individuals besides the twelve are specifically referred to as apostles (Paul, Silas, and Timothy - 1 Thessalonians 1: 1, 2:6; Apollos - 1 Corinthians 4:6,9; Barnabas - Acts 14:14; James - Galatians 1:19; Epaphroditus - Philippians 2:25; Junia and Andronicus - Romans 16:7). I like to call this level of apostleship the apostles of the Ascended Christ.

The apostles are the stewards of this heavenly dream for the world. They carry the heartbeat. They have the blueprints. The apostles are coming! If you don't know an apostle, don't worry, that won't last. God is going to release many apostles in the days ahead. Here is the heart of an apostle:

> Him we preach, warning every man and teaching every man in all wisdom, that we may present every man *perfect in Christ Jesus.* To this end I also labor, striving according to His working which works in me mightily. (Colossians 1:28,29, emphasis mine)

> "My little children, for whom I labor in birth again *until Christ is formed in you...*" (Galatians 4:19, emphasis mine)

> "But we all, with unveiled faces, beholding as in a mirror the glory of the Lord, are *being transformed into the same image* from glory to glory, just as by the Spirit of the Lord." (2 Corinthians 3:18, emphasis mine)

Paul writes in Ephesians about the church when he says:

"Which is His body, *the fullness of Him* who fills all in all." (1:23)

"…'Till we all come to the unity of the faith and of the knowledge of the Son of God, *to a perfect man, to the measure of the stature of the fullness of Christ.*" (4:13)

"…That He might present her to *Himself a glorious church, not having spot or wrinkle or any such thing,* but that she should be holy and without blemish." (5:27)

The apostles understand this dream and it is what drives them. The church will look like Jesus. This is how God will show the world who He is. "For whom He foreknew, He also predestined to be conformed to the image of His Son, that He might be the firstborn among many brethren." (Romans 8:29) Jesus will have a family of brothers and sisters in the earth that carry a resemblance to Him. This is as certain as God lives!

For this dream of God's to come true, there are some changes that are going to have to take place. Believers in Jesus will have to emerge from behind the closed doors of the "church" sub-culture, and live out their faith daily as a part of real life. Outside the walls of institutional religion there are many people who are searching for truth and spiritual reality. They may not know it yet, but they are waiting for you. They are waiting to see the only Jesus that they may ever get to see.

The apostolic dream cannot be fulfilled with the prevalent traditional ideas of church. Many of these people find "church" to be irrelevant to their lives and are resistant to its restrictive structure. If we are infected with the dream to have Jesus plainly seen and authentically represented to people in search of Him, it will inevitably lead us out. We must follow Jesus. Jesus has left the building.

CHAPTER FOUR

THE RELIGIOUS SPIRIT

This is what rock star Bono said in an interview with Oprah Winfrey on September 20, 2002: "I grew up in Ireland. My father was Catholic and my mother was Protestant. I am a believer, but I learned to be somewhat skeptical of religion. Religion is that thing, when God (like Elvis) has left the building. But if God is in the house, you get something else." Yes, Bono inspired the title of this book. I could only dream of meeting him one day, to thank him in person for the insight. Jesus and religion couldn't be further apart on the spectrum. One of the greatest enemies to Jesus' motivations is the religious spirit.

It was a beautiful Friday afternoon in September. I had just settled into my room at the house where I was staying in Decorah, Iowa. I was tired from the travels, so I decided I would take a little nap before the conference started. I was the guest speaker for the weekend, and I wasn't quite sure what the Lord wanted me to say. I was hoping He would soon give me the message. Unsurprisingly, sleep overtook prayer, so I sunk into the blankets.

Sometime later, towards the end of my nap, I entered into that state where you're stuck somewhere between the dream world and being awake. I could hear people in other parts of the house but was still in sleep mode. It was then that God's emphatic statement rushed into my thoughts. "A religious spirit has fallen upon this region like a blanket. This is how to defeat it: Read the story of David dancing in the streets."

As soon as this entered my heart, I was instantly awake. I quickly wrote it down and looked up the passage where David returned the ark of the covenant back to Jerusalem, and danced through the streets in celebration. I found it in 2 Samuel, chapter six.

THE GLORY BOX

Several decades had passed since the active presence of God had been in its rightful place at the heart of the nation of Israel. The ark of the Lord was Israel's most precious possession. But it was captured by their dreadful enemy, the Philistines (See 1 Samuel 4:10, 11). The people of Israel were mortified.

The ark was usually at home in the tabernacle of Moses at Shiloh, within a room called the Holy of Holies. It was a box covered with gold, and the lid of the box was called the Mercy Seat. On the top of it stood two golden cherubim, one on each end of the Mercy Seat, with their faces bowed down and the tips of their wings almost touching. The ark contained a copy of the Ten Commandments, which summarized the covenant God made with Moses and the people of Israel. God's manifest presence loomed over the Mercy Seat. The people considered it to be the place where God lived. Now it was gone.

The Philistines took the ark to a city called Ashdod and placed it in their temple near the idol of their false god "Dagon." (1 Samuel 5:1-7) Dagon means "fish," and was represented by human hands and face, with a fish's body. In the morning when the priests of Dagon entered the temple, they found to their utter horror the statue of Dagon fallen down with its face at the foot of the ark. They raised the idol up back to its place of honor, only to find it fallen again the next morning. This time the idol's extremities were broken off, leaving the stump or "fishy" part of him. Plagues and boils broke out among the Philistines. This "box" was more trouble then it was worth. After seven months of being passed around between a few of the Philistine cities, suffering the same outcome in each one, the ark was finally put on a cart, pulled by oxen, and sent on its way out of their country. It was brought to the house of an Israelite man by the name Abinadab. (1 Samuel 6:1-12, 13-20)

Over seventy years later, after David had become the King of Israel, it was in the heart of David to travel to the house of Abinadab so that he might bring back the glory of God into his city. Even now, thousands of years later, there are many men and women all over the earth with this same desire and passion. Like David of old, they have a heart after God's own heart, and they long to see God's active presence come to their city and nation.

A HARD LESSON

David brought together thirty thousand of his most prominent men and leaders in the nation to retrieve the ark from its place at the house of Abinadab in the region of Baale Judah. Thousands upon thousands of people came out that day to watch this procession. They rested the ark on a new cart pulled by oxen, and the sons of Abinadab, Uzzah and Ahio drove the cart. Things were off to a great start. There was joy and celebration as David and all the house of Israel played music before the Lord on all kinds of instruments. The nation was united. This marked a day in history that would never be forgotten. This is the kind of event you tell your grandchildren about. "I was there when the ark of the Lord was brought into the City of David. I saw it with my own eyes."

Everything was going as planned, and David was ecstatic. His dream was unfolding right before his eyes. Then suddenly, without any warning, tragedy struck.

At a certain point on the road, near Nachon's threshing floor, the oxen stumbled and the cart shook. Uzzah, thinking that the ark was going to fall, put out his hand to steady it. As he touched the ark of the Lord, something happened that nobody expected. 2 Samuel 6:7 reports, "Then the anger of the Lord was aroused against Uzzah, and God struck him there for his error; and he died there by the ark of God."

What? How could this be? In a moment, the sound of thousands of people laughing, singing, dancing and shouting was reduced to dead silence. David was absolutely devastated. The Scripture goes on to describe how David was angry with the Lord, and also afraid of Him. In desperation, David cried out, "How will the ark of the Lord come to me?" They sent the crowds home, and put the ark in the backyard of a house nearby. The home belonged to Obed-Edom. It stayed there for three months, while David mourned and attempted to figure out what went wrong.

This is a powerful and sobering story about carrying the presence and glory of God. David soon discovered that "no one may carry the ark of God but the Levites, for the Lord has chosen them to carry the ark of God and to minister before Him forever." (1 Chronicles 15:2) The "glory box" was never meant to be carried by a cart and oxen. This is what the Philistines did, and David along with the House of Israel copied the methods of this foreign nation, instead of doing things the way God had instructed.

God is very particular about how His glory should be handled. Our man-made ideas and methods won't cut it. A cart and an ox can be very useful, but it may not be used to carry the glory of God. Our church programs, buildings, crusades, websites, TV ministries or any other tools we have created will never be able to adequately convey the knowledge of the glory of God's person and awesome power. This is a privilege reserved only for priests. We are the priesthood of God. All those who put their trust in Jesus are called "a royal priesthood." (1 Peter 2:9) We are the glory carriers. Remember the apostolic dream and Numbers 14:21. Remember the principle of "incarnation." The ones driving the carts had better be very careful.

I'm not referring here to motive. David's motive was pure. David had the right idea, but was doing it the wrong way. He only failed to consult the Lord for His guidance and proper order of things. (See 1 Chronicles 15:13) In our zeal we often neglect to seek God for the "how." We must learn the lost art of waiting on God. As priests, our role is to "minister before Him forever." That Hebrew word is *sharat* which means to wait on, to serve, to attend. God may put something in our heart to do for Him, but we must wait for Him to make the first move. We must listen carefully to how He wants this thing done, and obey Him precisely as He orders it.

Thousands of pastors and church leaders drop out of ministry or change churches every year in North America. Perhaps this is partly the Lord's doing. Is God displeased about all the stuff we are doing that He didn't tell us to do? How much of the busyness in the church is actually His will and born out of the leading of His Spirit? It is my experience that the abundance of activity going on is actually a hindrance to hearing and waiting on God. If you're not sure that God wants you to do what you're doing, then stop and wait on Him.

Have you noticed that our state-of-the-art gospel presentations or new innovative evangelistic gimmicks really don't touch people? Most people come to Christ the good old-fashioned way, someone they know showed them Jesus. God wants to be carried by flesh and blood. We cannot be replaced by technology in this area. Human contact is how God gets close to people. He longs to reveal His heart in an intimate way, through you and me.

WATCH YOUR STEP

Let's try again. David went back to the house of Obed-Edom and made sure things were right this time. He instructed the Levites to bear the ark and as they proceeded he had them stop on the sixth step. On every sixth step, they sacrificed "oxen and fatted sheep." David was almost over-paranoid about messing this up again. He wanted to make sure they were still connected to God in their journey along the way. The number six in biblical symbolism is the number representing man. Before we get too far walking in the ways of man, this story is reminding us to be diligent and to wait on the Lord.

We must watch our step. It can be tricky to walk upright in this world that we live in. The world and its system are definitely against us. 1 John 2:16 defines the spirit of the world as being *lust, lust,* and *pride.* There is a picture in the book of Revelation of a scarlet harlot sitting on the beast and "the inhabitants of the earth were made drunk with the wine of her fornication." (See Revelation 17:2) She calls out to us every moment of every day that we're out there. "Come and drink!" Lust and fornication is the spirit behind the culture. Be careful. Watch your step.

As bad as this is, there is a more sinister evil waiting to ensnare you.

It is much more subtle, and it masquerades itself as being from God. It is rooted in lust and pride, but extremely difficult to detect. I am speaking of the religious spirit. Religion is the worst matrix of all! Religion is dangerous because it makes you think you're okay when you're not. Not long ago an unbelieving friend of mine asked me what I thought the most deceptive religion was. I answered, "Christianity." I could tell that he was shocked by my answer. Any "Christian tradition" that comes across in a pharisaical stance but calls it "Jesus," is more deadly than openly "anti-Christian" sentiment. The religious spirit is extremely deceptive. It even persecutes the things God cares about, in the name of "God." Most people who are bound by this evil spirit don't even know it.

The scariest passage in the Bible is Matthew 7:21-23:

> Many will say to Me in that day, 'Lord, Lord, have we not prophe-
> sied in Your name, cast out demons in Your name, and done many
> wonders in Your name?' And then I will declare to them, 'I
> never knew you; depart from Me, you who practice lawlessness!'

Doing things for God, even supernatural things, doesn't mean that you know Jesus and Jesus knows you. In the end, it's all about relationship with Jesus. Religion can't give you that. A religious spirit will actually hinder relationship with God, and make you think that God is on your side. It's a nasty thing.

When I say "religious spirit," I'm talking about a work of deception perpetrated by evil, which gives the person plagued by it a certain air of self-righteousness, but it's more than attitude. It is a spiritual oppression that attacks the individual's motivation under the surface. A major hint at identifying a religious spirit is that a religious spirit will always highlight the means to an end, and lose sight of the desired outcome. The means becomes the end. Let me give you a few examples to clarify this point.

Jesus, in John 5:39, told the Pharisees that they searched the Scripture diligently; thinking that in the pages of Scripture there is eternal life. However, Jesus said that the Scriptures speak about Him, but that they wouldn't come to Him that they may have life. The Scriptures are a means to an end. They have been given to us to point the way to the One they speak of. However, the Pharisees couldn't see beyond the Scriptures. Reading and studying the Bible became an act of religious duty that lost its purpose of knowing God more.

I often use the illustration of a menu. When you go to a restaurant to eat, they give you a menu full of items to order. You could read the menu, study the menu, and know that menu from cover to cover. What if you gathered with some friends to talk about the menu together, and even sing a few songs about it? You could go all over town spreading the news of how great that menu is, but at the end of the day, you're still hungry. The menu is a means to an end. The menu is useless unless you order the food that it describes and eat.

The Pharisees were students of the Old Testament, and they had "Ph.D.s" in the Law. However, the means became the end to them. They convinced themselves to be satisfied with the menu without needing to order and eat.

If you are a "good Christian," you read your Bible, pray everyday and go to church every Sunday. Have you ever stopped to ask why? (There's that question again.) These things may serve a purpose in helping us to grow in the knowledge of God but are still only a means to that end.

The end goal is to know Him. Don't feel guilty because you don't do these things. If you do feel guilt, you may be in the grips of a religious spirit. Remember the "Lord, Lord" people.

When religion takes something positive such as reading the Bible and gets its grubby little paws all over it, the religious spirit empties it of its power. Reading the Bible becomes stressful. Will you get something out of it? Why does it seem so dry? Are you reading for the sake of getting your quota in? Is this your duty? Or do you want to know God more and experience the things that you are reading?

Another example is the Sabbath. Take one day a week to rest, be with your family and with the Lord. God instituted the Sabbath for humanity's own good and pleasure. After the religious leaders of Jesus' day got through with it, people were now "made for the Sabbath." The servant becomes the master in religion. There was no rest for people on the Sabbath anymore. They were too fearful of breaking it. Any little thing would be misconstrued by the religious as "working on the Sabbath." Jesus was criticized for healing people on the Sabbath. What's wrong with this picture? The means became the end once again.

Why do you do everything you do for God? You have to know. The Scripture says, "Examine yourself as to whether you are in the faith." (2 Corinthians 13:5) If there is anything you do religiously and you are not getting to know Him better through it, then stop doing it. I mean stop it cold turkey, even if it's something you're "supposed to do" to be a good Christian. If you're trying to be a "good" Christian, stop! You are in grave danger. You need to fall in love with Jesus again or maybe for the first time.

When you're in love, you don't "have to" do anything. You want to do what pleases the one you love. Going to church, reading your Bible, praying, worshipping in song and all that we as Christians tend to do; it all means nothing to God if the heart is not there. He would rather you not do it at all. Take a break. Come back to it again when the coast is clear. Get connected with Jesus. Don't let the religious spirit rob you of your relationship with God.

RETALIATION

We should probably get back to the story in 2 Samuel 6. David and all the house of Israel had one major party. The ark was success-fully brought into Jerusalem to the tabernacle David had erected for it. David was so full of joy and praise that he literally stripped down to his "linen ephod" and danced through the streets. In our day, it would be equivalent to seeing the Prime Minister or President in his undershirt and boxers. The linen ephod was a priest's undergarments.

David danced before the Lord with all his might, twirling and spinning round and round. The dream of his heart had come true that day. He turned to the people and blessed them. He sent them all home with a loaf of bread, a piece of meat, and a raisin cake.

The religious spirit in this story of David is represented by David's wife, Michal, and her reaction to David's freedom in God. There are three things that she does that are classic symptoms of religiosity. Now, this story serves as an illustration and there is nothing in the text that says that she had a "religious spirit." However, I will show you how each of these traits in Michal can also be seen in the Pharisees, who indeed were very religious.

First of all, she was nowhere to be found. This was the most signifi-cant event of her lifetime and she stayed home. She did look through her window from a distance, and was extremely embarrassed by her husband. The record shows that "she despised him in her heart," because of the *spinning around in your underwear* public display.

A religious spirit will always distance itself from the things God is doing, and more specifically, from the people Jesus loves. The Pharisees didn't get what Jesus was doing. "Why do you eat with sinners?" they would ask Him. Tax-collectors, prostitutes and drunkards weren't appropriate acquaintances for a "rabbi." The word "Pharisee" comes from a root word that means "to separate." The Pharisees separated themselves from the people that Jesus loved, using their own sense of self-righteousness as a standard of measure.

I learned that the religious leaders of Jesus' time had some personal rules concerning how to define what a "sinner" was. If you talked to a woman in public, you would be considered a sinner. If a Pharisee saw a prostitute in near vicinity, he was to gather up his priestly robes, put his hand to his mouth and gasp in disgust. This was how they let everyone know that they were having no relations with the sinful woman. If you had any dealings with Samaritans or ever ate with a Gentile, you would be a sinner. Lepers were sinners and if you touched them you would be too. If you touched the sick at all, you would be considered a sinner by contamination.

Jesus broke all their rules. He didn't let religiosity stop Him from loving the ones that needed Him most. Jesus broke two rules in one episode when He spoke with a Samaritan woman in public. He let a prostitute kiss his feet with her adulterous lips. He watched while she washed them with her own tears, and dried them with her beautiful long hair (an asset in her profession). She poured perfume on Him, the very perfume she would use to help her lure the men to her bed. With these "sinful" things, she worshipped Him and repented. It was all she had. It was her life. In Jesus a sinner can touch the ark, the very glory of God.

It was because of incidents like these that they plotted how they might destroy Jesus. Jesus was rejected by the chief priests because of the company He kept, and it ultimately put Him on the cross.

The religious spirit is dangerous and very violent. It can take otherwise normally "nice" people and turn them into vicious attackers. This is why Jesus often told the people He healed to keep quiet about it. It could be extremely dangerous to share this with the wrong people. Jesus did this in fulfillment of a prophecy in Isaiah, "He will not quarrel nor cry out, nor will anyone hear His voice in the streets. A bruised reed He will not break, and smoking flax He will not quench." (Matthew 12: 15-21)

Jesus avoided conflict with the religious spirit as much as He could, until His final week. In Jerusalem, He came on strong with the "Woes to the Scribes and Pharisees." (Matthew 23) He was crucified within days.

Please, if you're in an environment riddled with a "religious spirit," run for your life. You may not be killed physically, but you are in trouble spiritually, emotionally, and mentally. Don't fall for the illusion that you can be an agent of change. I've never seen nor heard of that happening. Either your fire and zeal will be quenched or your tender branch will be snapped. Hide from the religious spirit. It is more powerful than you could imagine. It seems like everybody has some "horror" story of church. This is why millions of young people in the West have left organized religion. It is survival.

Not only did Michal keep herself at a distance, but she was very concerned about what people thought of her husband and, by implication, herself. Sarcastically, she said to David, "How glorious was the king of Israel today, uncovering himself today in the eyes of the maids of his servants." (2 Samuel 6:20) What did all the young ladies think of her husband? What do people think of me?

The religious spirit is obsessively preoccupied with appearances. It is rooted in a fear of man rather than a fear of God. Everything the Pharisees did, they did for others to see. Jesus taught us to do what we do so that only God the Father would see. (See Matthew 6:1-18) Jesus said of the Pharisees that they only kept the outside of their cup clean and were like white-washed tombs. They appeared beautiful and clean outwardly, but full of dead men's bones within. (See Matthew 23:25-28) They kept up with their appearances, but secretly were evil.

It seems like you can't do both. You must either focus on the outward appearance or on the heart. If you're determined to keep the outward expression looking "righteous," then your inside will be filled with evil and secret sin. Keep your heart after God and let Jesus take care of how others perceive you.

Religiosity's obsession with appearances leads to hypocrisy. You cannot be a follower of Jesus if you hold the opinion of others in high regard. (Galatians 1:10) Being afraid of what people think of you, especially the religious, will catch you in a web of deceit. I think of Peter who ate with Paul's Gentile friends until the Jewish brothers from Jerusalem came around. When Peter saw them, he withdrew from the Gentiles, because of what these "false brothers" might have thought of him. Paul didn't tolerate this for a moment, and corrected Peter to his face publicly. (Galatians 2:1-6, 11-13)

Paul's response to Peter echoes David's response to his wife. He told her that what he did that day was "before the Lord" and that he would be even "more undignified" than this. (What is more undignified than twirling in the streets in your under garments? I don't want to picture it.) The point was, David was not letting his wife make him second guess the authentic expression of worship that was coming out of him that day. He didn't for one moment let the tentacles of religiosity and the fear of man pull him into bondage.

You have to resist religiosity or it will get you. You mustn't do something or not do something because of fear of what people may think of you. Whatever you do, do it before the Lord. David didn't care what the young ladies thought. He didn't care what the thousands of people in the street thought. He didn't even care what his own wife thought. He had his eyes on only one person that day: The Lord.

Finally, a religious spirit thinks highly of itself. Michal was annoyed that David presented himself as a "base fellow" or common man. David was better than this. He was the most prominent man in the land. His reputation as a powerful and wise leader was known throughout the world. Why was he allowing himself to get so low? He took off all that distinguished him as king. Off went the crown and the kingly apparel. He was reduced to a simple priest. I can't help but think that David was a type of Christ, who also left His position in glory and humbled Himself to become a man. (Philippians 2)

The Pharisees loved the public places of honor. They also relished the praise of men and they loved to be addressed with titles such as "rabbi." Being in this elevated position gave them a sense of power over others. They would judge others by their own measuring sticks. Read this parable spoken by Jesus:

And He spoke this parable to some who trusted in themselves

that they were righteous, and despised others: "Two men went up to the temple to pray, one a Pharisee and the other a tax collector. The Pharisee stood and prayed thus with himself, 'God, I thank You that I am not like other men—extortioners, unjust, adulterers, or even as this tax collector. I fast twice a week; I give tithes of all that I possess.' And the tax collector, standing afar off, would not so much as raise his eyes to Heaven, but beat his breast, saying, 'God be merciful to me a sinner!' I tell you, this man went down to his house justified rather than the other; for everyone who exalts himself will be humbled, and he who humbles himself will be exalted." (Luke 18:9-14)

YOU SHALL BE BARREN!

We now come down to the climax of this story, which is rather shocking to say the least. David didn't succumb to his wife's pressure to doubt his act of extravagant worship. As a direct result of Michal's attitude towards David, the Scripture tells us that Michal had no children to the day of her death.

When I read this those words stood out. The secret to defeating the religious spirit was hidden here in this verse. Then God showed me that the only way the religious spirit could maintain its hold over time in a family or a church or even a community, was to pass it on from generation to generation.

The Pharisees had disciples. These were spiritual sons. Jesus called the Scribes "the blind leading the blind." Jesus said, "The disciple becomes like his teacher." (Luke 6:37-42) Religion breeds and infects the next generation with its venom. Jesus observed that the Pharisees would travel to faraway countries to win a single convert, and when they do, they heap so much legalism on his back that they make him two times the son of hell that they are. (Matthew 23:15) The religious spirit maintains its grip and influence by passing it on from fathers to children, and the cycle continues.

What if God were to curse the religious spirit with spiritual barrenness? What would that look like? What would that mean? Perhaps the emerging generations would have some kind of immunity to its poison. Somehow "religion" just wouldn't stick to them. I don't quite understand how it all works, but I believe God is saying to the religious spirit in the older generation, "You shall not have children in the next generation!"

THE EMERGING GENERATION HOLDS A KEY

Understanding what the Spirit of God is doing in the emerging generations is critical to having our grids changed for the new wine that is coming. Knowing that this generation may possess some kind of vaccination to religiosity gives us a clue pointing towards the reasons why they may be the ones to break the old wineskin.

Recently, I was invited to be the speaker at a youth camp primarily aimed at ages 13 to 18. There were about 120 kids involved and these young people were amazing. I so enjoyed being with them. I know it was as much a blessing for me as it was for them. There was a young woman at the camp who had badly sprained her ankle. She had to walk with crutches as a result. When I saw her sitting at a picnic table one day, I noticed she was in pain. Something unusual for me these days emerged from the depths of my heart. I wanted to see God heal her.

To be honest, I didn't have the courage to tell her this although I did offer to pray for her. The next evening as I was praying about what God wanted me to share with the youth, He spoke to me. God instructed me to tell the young people about all my experiences in God as a teenager during the Come to the Cross movement. The Lord told me that He wanted to pour out His Spirit on the youth and release healing. When He showed me this, my heart was overwhelmed with God's kindness. I told the Lord that I would try to follow only His leading. I wasn't going to suggest anything to the kids. God would have to do it. I wasn't interested in trying to make things happen or pump up the crowd. After the message that night, I invited the youth to come forward to receive the power of the Holy Spirit in their lives. Instantly, over a hundred kids rushed toward me and pinned me to the stage for almost three hours.

It was amazing and something that I hadn't seen in more than ten years. It started with tears flowing down many of the kids' faces. Then the healing began. The young lady on crutches was healed. It started a chain reaction where we all witnessed at least fifteen healings take place before our eyes, including the measurable and visible disappearance of scoliosis. Not only did physical healings occur, but deep emotional wounds were touched. Young men and women confessed their sin to one another, along with their fears and needs. It seemed to me like everyone was crying at one point or another.

It was hard to track all that was happening. Some kids were prophesying, while others received the gift of tongues, and still others were caught in a deep place of intercession and prayer. It was all going on at the same time. God was just pouring out his blessing upon this group. I was so touched by the sincerity and purity of these young people.

There were many who gave their lives to Christ that night, because God became real to them.

These young people came from Christian traditions that do not normally experience or expect these kinds of supernatural activities to happen today. The churches involved with this camp definitely belonged to the more conservative wing of evangelical Christian culture. Although you may expect to hear about this sort of thing happening perhaps in Pentecostal or charismatic circles, no such denomination was present. Some of the youth pastors approached me afterward and told me they'd never seen anything like this before. One young leader had read about experiences like this, but this was the first time he had seen it with his own eyes. Although the leaders anticipated a possible unfavorable reaction from the religious environments of their home churches, the young people themselves couldn't care less.

These precious teens seemed to hold no allegiance to their denominational backgrounds. They were not polluted with theological arguments stating that God does not act like He once did in the book of Acts. Furthermore, when they looked at one another, no such labels as Baptist, Wesleyan, or Presbyterian existed. They were one, much like another group of 120 believers in an upper room so very long ago. (See Acts chapters 1 and 2) They do not deny their experience. It won't be taken away from them. The religious spirit has no seed in them. They seem to be immune.

CHAPTER FIVE

EMERGING (OR HIDDEN) GENERATION?

"YOU MEANT EVIL AGAINST ME, BUT GOD MEANT IT FOR GOOD."

Joseph was one of twelve sons of the patriarch Jacob. His father loved him more than his brothers. To show this love, he gave Joseph a beautiful coat of many colors as a gift and favored him above his other sons. You can find this story in the thirty-seventh chapter of Genesis.

Joseph's siblings were extremely jealous of him. Jealousy became hatred when Joseph foolishly shared his dreams with them. He was seventeen years old when God began to reveal his destiny to him in two prophetic dreams. Both implied that his family would one day bow down to him.

One morning as Joseph went out into the fields to find his brothers, everything he knew was about to change. Through the envy and evil intent of his brothers, the ones closest to him, Joseph experienced something that my generation knows all too well. Three evil plots were released against him for his demise. It is these same things that have been a plague to the emerging generation. We are "Joseph."

I say "we" because I am a member of the emerging generation. My parents are "Baby Boomers," and that makes me belong to "Generation X." Most people are already familiar with the terms. For the sake of those who are not sure, I will briefly define them. Traditionally, these groups are identified by the range of years that the births occurred. The Baby Boom generation refers to the post-WW2 explosion of babies that lasted for nineteen years (1946 through 1964). Comparatively, from 1965 to 1984 there were considerably fewer babies being born here in North America, thus the "Baby Bust." However, in my opinion, a generation is a group that has experienced the same time period in history, when certain shared events forge into their minds and hearts a common mindset and identity. Therefore, more accurately defined, "Baby Boomer" or "Baby Buster" is an attitude, a worldview. Although it does not describe everyone born between the specified years and does express a subculture of that group, these mindsets tend to remain extremely pervasive.

The Baby Bust generation, or just "busters," has also been termed "baby bummers," "twenty-nothings," "slackers," the "Repair Generation," the "Marginalized Generation," the "Recovering Generation," the "Surviving Generation," the "MTV Generation," and the "Generation After." Then there's "Generation X," the title attached to my age bracket by Douglas Coupland in his 1991 novel *Generation X: Tales for an Accelerated Culture*. We actually resent every one of these labels; however, for the purpose of identification I will reluctantly refer to my generation as Gen X.

First, when Joseph's brothers saw him approaching, they said to one another, "Look! Here comes the dreamer," and they plotted to kill him. Can you imagine that? How could family scheme to terminate one of its own, to purposely end a life? What kind of evil is this that the ones you trust the most intend on getting rid of you? There are explanations as to why Generation X in North America is considerably smaller than the Baby Boomer generation. We are the first generation with mothers on the pill.

Many of us were not wanted. For those who weren't prevented from being conceived, abortion became a convenient "choice." There has never been a more aborted generation in history, with an average of 1.3 million babies destroyed in the U.S. every year. Forty-seven million of my fellow revolutionaries in America alone never made it past the womb.[1] I too almost became prey to this vicious enemy. My parents conceived me out of wedlock and were advised by relatives to abort me. I thank God that I was fortunate to have parents who wanted me in the face of tremendous pressure from all sides. I escaped.

For those of us who survived the first attack, the second strike came with debilitating force. The brothers decided not to kill Joseph, but fueled by their hatred, stripped him of his coat. This coat was the symbol of his father's love and approval. We have grown up in a world without fathers. We have been stripped of the father's affection and influence.

We are the victims of divorce, the children of broken homes. We are the "fatherless generation." Half of us experienced the deep pain that comes when Mom and Dad "stop loving each other." Divorce breeds confusion when it comes to being able to relate to God as our Father. I have friends that have to endure the drama of four or five Christmas family dinners, in an attempt to see each branch of the family. This is the generation that has spent the other weekend at their other parent's home, redefining the concept of family with relationships such as "dad's girlfriend," "mom's previous ex-husband," "my second step-father," and "my step-brother's father's ex-wife."

As a by-product of broken homes, this generation fears loneliness the most. We long to fit in somewhere. I believe this is one reason why the

71

sit-com "Friends" was so popular. It expresses the deep desire and long-ing in the hearts of an entire generation. Here you have six young men and women who live in each other's space. This explains why we love to get together in small groups of friends, united by common interest and mutual acceptance. These small groups act as surrogate families.

Even for the families that managed to stay together, often both parents were working for more material possessions or off "finding themselves." We are the "latch-key kids." We would come home after school with a key to the house around our neck. We let ourselves in, made a sandwich, and watched TV. My favorite after-school show was "Happy Days." Fonzie was my role model. The Cunninghams became the dream family.

It's always about fathers. For every messed up person you see in the world, there often is an abusive or absent father partly to blame. All of us need a good one, but they are hard to come by. My own father is one of the best. I am one of the fortunate ones. Yet as a young man, some-thing inside me longed for a spiritual father, someone to help me grow and mature in the faith.

I have no doubt that God led me to such a person. He was a promi-nent church leader in our city, a man of prayer, who carried fatherly authority. Things were wonderful in the beginning. For two years I apprenticed under him, admired him, and sought for his approval and praise. The risk of putting your life in the hands of mortal men opens a person up to a great potential for pain and disillusionment. Although I indeed got hurt, I know it was not this man's intention. Our relationship broke down primarily because of our inability to understand the differ-ence in mindset between his generation and mine.

A few years ago, some of the old gang from my youth came together and we shared our stories with one another. It seemed like most of us had gone through a sort of "wilderness" period, in the days since Come to the Cross. The common experience that we all shared was a feeling of neglect and abandonment from our spiritual fathers. We longed for their affection and for personal relationship, but discovered that we were mere appointments in their day-timers. We found in them a reluctance to share what they had with us. They also seemed threatened and resistant to the new ideas and values that we possessed. Our mentoring relationships came to a halt, leaving us still with a feeling of being spiritually "fatherless."

I believe that it is the role of the father to instill a sense of destiny in the heart of his child. Fathers give their children the self-confidence and esteem needed to attain their dreams. Now that I have children, I desire to help them discover their calling and define their identity. When both my sons were newborn babies, I held each one up in the air, much like the opening scene of the Disney movie *The Lion King*, and exclaimed, "Lord, use him!" If you are fatherless, let the words in this book reach you. Let God, Your Father, hold you in His arms and speak of His faith in you and His ability to make your life count for something wonderful.

Finally, Joseph's brothers threw him into a pit and sold him to traveling merchants. He was devalued, banished from his home, and cast down to a place of hopelessness and despair. He became a slave, the very bottom of the economic and social structure of his day. The next fourteen years of Joseph's life went from bad to worse, until finally he found himself in the dungeon of Pharaoh's palace in Egypt, paying for a crime he did not commit.

As a generation, just like Joseph, the things that have come against us have positioned us in just the right place. Joseph was closer to his destiny in that Egyptian prison than he would have been if he were still in his homeland with his family. He was given the opportunity to speak to the ruler of the world and demonstrate his spiritual insight and wisdom. In just one day, Joseph was promoted from lawbreaker to the second-in-command of all of Egypt. The Scriptures tell us that the entire world came to Joseph to buy grain. Likewise, the ultimate impact of this "Joseph generation" today will be on a global scale, the gospel touching all nations.

It is amazing to me how God used the trials of Joseph's life to propel him into his mission. In later years, Joseph had two sons. Their names had special meaning. He called his first-born "Manasseh" signifying that God had made him "forget all the toil and all his father's house." He named his second son Ephraim, which means "God has caused me to be fruitful in the land of my affliction." These are two incredible promises of hope and healing for my generation. Joseph eventually reconciled with his brothers and told them, "It was not you who sent me here, but God." (Genesis 45:8) Joseph came face to face with the sovereignty of God.

It is my prayer for the emerging generations that they too would see what Joseph saw. Our troubles have placed us in just the right spot, at just the right time. We are in the hands of God. He is going to take what was meant for harm and use it for good. He does this all the time. He loves to confound the strong and the wise of this world by using weak and foolish people. This generation will be used by God to set the stage that will bring about a global revelation of Jesus. The world is in famine, and in a split second, Joseph will emerge from out of nowhere to take his place. "But as for you, you meant evil against me; but God meant it for good, in order to bring it about as it is this day, to save many people alive." (Genesis 50:20)

STILL IN HIDING

Where is this emerging generation? There seems to be no sign of this alleged group of revolutionaries anywhere. Most of them are not in churches where you would imagine them to be. If what I am saying about this special generation is true, you would think they would be emerging out of the church, where they have prepared and trained for this great mandate that is upon them. However, most of them have left the (church) building, and many of them appear uninterested and apathetic when it comes to religion.

They do not hold the visible positions of leadership and authority. They are nameless and faceless. They live in the shadows. They are in hiding. You can find them in cafés, lounges, homes and apartments, restaurants, or anywhere a few friends can come together to connect in casual dialogue over a cup of gourmet coffee. These are unusual places to find the ones that will change the face of Christianity.

God likes to hide stuff. I am not talking about covering up sin or lying to avoid getting caught. I am referring to keeping a precious thing hidden, so that those who would seek to destroy it would not be able to find it. Jesus spoke in parables to conceal the truth of the kingdom from those whose hearts were hard. The kingdom of God is like a treasure "hidden" in a field. Jesus instructed us to "not give what is holy to the dogs; nor cast your pearls before swine, lest they trample them under their feet, and turn and tear you in pieces." (Matthew 7:6) In this way, I believe that God is hiding my generation. Joseph was safer hidden in that dungeon in Egypt than he was with his brothers.

My generation does not feel safe in the church as an institution. We are hiding from it. We have been misunderstood and rejected by it. We live in the world, and the world has taught us. Egypt, in the Scriptures, represents the world and its system. Joseph hid in Egypt. Moses was hidden in the heart of Egypt when a decree was given to kill all first-born Hebrew sons under the age of two. When Jesus' young life was in danger from a similar command given by King Herod, the angel told Joseph and Mary to take the boy to Egypt. Whenever there is such a slaughter of children as seen with Moses' and Jesus' generations, it is a sign that Satan is out to destroy the deliverance that is in that generation. My generation has suffered many casualties of this demonic attack. The devil is after this army of revolutionaries, but God is hiding them where He always does, in Egypt.

The tension between "organized religion" and the emergence of the "organic church" is like what was going on between King Saul and David. King Saul represents the "establishment" that is threatened by new leadership (David), who is anointed by God to serve a new generation. For a season, King Saul pursued David around the wilderness seeking to kill him. For a time, David found his home among the Philistines. He too was safer in a pagan land than with his own people. David finally found a place to hide in a cave called Adullam. (1 Samuel 22:1, 2) While he was there, his parents discovered where he was staying and they came to him with four hundred other rejects of society.

These individuals were in distress, in debt, and discontented. They were hurt and bitter in their souls. That was the beginning of the world-renowned "David's Mighty Men." From this small band of misfits came a powerful army. Today, there is another cave of Adullam attracting and hiding the disconnected of my generation. They are full of pain and disenfranchised. God sees them as mighty men and women, and they will inherit the earth.

THE POSTMODERN PLANET

Western culture is in a period of great flux. The last few decades have introduced us to a critical change in worldview. Much of Europe has already made this transition, and North America has quickly caught up to speed. We cannot adequately describe characteristics of the emerging generations without considering the major paradigm shift that has given birth to their corporate identity. I am referring to the move from "modernism" to "postmodernism."

The modern era began at the death of the Middle Ages and the birth of the Renaissance. Modernity reached its pinnacle in the Age of Enlightenment, a European intellectual movement of the seventeenth and eighteenth centuries. The Enlightenment period celebrated human reason and values. Intellect and logic were superior to emotion and subjective experience. Reality was defined by its measurability in a laboratory. If it couldn't be seen, heard, smelled, tasted or touched, it wasn't "real."

The empirical method became the litmus test of truth. Anything supernatural, extraterrestrial, or paranormal simply did not exist in the modern world. Christianity was rejected because it was falsely considered "unscientific" or "non-rational." Eventually, men like C.S. Lewis and other apologists rose up to the challenge, proving that science and logic were compatible with Christian faith. Things were different in modern society. Families were more functional, decisions were simpler, traditions continued unquestioned, the future looked bright, and issues were black and white. There is a right answer and there is a wrong answer (And *I'm* right!).

The Modern world is a different planet from the one my generation lives on. The emerging generations are "postmodern" all the way. Sometime shortly after the dawn of the twentieth century, the modern era started crumbling, and by the 1980s it lay in ruins. Postmodernism is now our operating system. It is the lens through which we see reality. So, what is it?

Postmodernism is defined by its distinction from modernity. On the postmodern planet, emotion and non-rational subjective experience reign supreme. Postmodernism says, "There is no such thing as absolute truth." An objective point of view does not exist. Postmoderns believe that we are the products of our environment. We are "social constructs," biased by our cultural predisposition. This worldview sees language as the fabric of what constitutes our truth, and language is culturally derived and can never be truly objective.

This philosophy maintains that all text is written with biases, and read and interpreted through personal experiential grids. Therefore, everything is relative. There is no absolute truth, only relative truth. In postmodernism, each person decides what is true for him or her. Have you ever heard someone say, "You have your truth and I have mine"? Welcome to the postmodern planet.

Postmoderns are extremely open to other points of view. Remember that they are seeking to experience truth for themselves. This makes them eager to hear your story and what you believe. They want to learn from others in order to assimilate different ideas into their own "pot-luck" belief system. However, there is one line that no one may cross.

On the postmodern planet, beware of the word "intolerant." Those who claim to have universal truth are seen as narrow, arrogant, and even dangerous. They are afraid that if you feel your beliefs are true for everyone, you may persecute those who do not believe as you do. Postmoderns cannot separate the person from the beliefs, since they were chosen or created by that person. Calling someone's beliefs wrong is an attack of that person. How many times have you heard someone in the church say, "Hate the sin, and love the sinner"? The natives of postmodernism do not believe that can be done. They feel that converting someone or evangelizing people groups is arrogant and wrong.

Before you join the cause to fight the force of postmodernism as some church leaders have resolved to do, consider for a moment the possibility it has presented to us. Postmodernism has fashioned my generation and has given us permission to pursue the meaning of life. It has given us a hunger for reality, our own reality. This emerging generation right around the world is ready for the apostolic dream. They are looking for authentic experience with Jesus.

Postmodern thinking people need to know truth for themselves. They are most impacted by truth that comes through experience and relationship. They must be able to say, "This is something that I know, not just what I read in a book." This is perfect, because salvation in Jesus itself hinges on an experience, a revelation of God. Young people are not looking to know more facts about God. They are looking to meet Him. They want to see Him active in the human experience. This becomes an open door for the gospel. It is a challenge to believers to live out their faith.

A MOVING TRAIN

I believe that postmodernism is a transitional cultural shift. This train that we are riding is going at light speed, covering vast distances, but only traveling a short period of time. I think at the most, it will last a few decades. Near the end of this book I will postulate what I believe will be our culture's post-"postmodern" movement. For now, I am talking about the emerging generations. In this metaphor of a train, each generation occupies one train car.

The postmodern train may only be two or three cars long. The first car contains my generation, Generation X. Similar attitudes also exist with the next generation often called Generation Y, and perhaps yet another generation. We are all on this train together, the emerging generations. I have specifically focused this study on Generation X for two reasons. First, Gen X typifies the postmodern identity, and serves as a model to bring understanding of that which is emerging. Secondly, I am writing from the place where I live, a Gen X'er myself.

WHY WE ARE HIDING FROM THE MODERN CHURCH

Now let's examine some characteristics possessed by the emerging generations that can paint a picture of exactly why we are hiding from the modern-driven church. These qualities are a product of shared social and cultural experiences, and the influences of postmodernism, as we have previously discussed.

I also want to note that the following values and descriptions were derived from firsthand experience. This is not based on generic statistical research, but as a result of personal relationship with the members of my generation. Besides, I have the inside scoop. As previously stated, I am an X'er. I am describing myself.

1. We fear our personal experience and feelings will be illegitimized by logic and reason.

If you happen to be an alien on my world from the planet "Modernity," you would say, "But this is so easy to refute." "Look at the circular reasoning." The postmodernist says, "There is no absolute truth." The modernist replies, "Is that statement true?" The postmodernist answers, "Yes, it's true." Then the logical modernist jumps up and exclaims, "If it's true that 'there is no absolute truth,' then the statement 'there is no absolute truth' is not true." The postmodern person at this point would just say, "Well that's what you believe." Are you shaking your head in confusion yet?

The point that I am trying to get across is that postmodernism does not really hold any water if your worldview is "modernism," because you can easily prove through logical arguments that postmodernism doesn't really make sense. However, the postmodernist has no concern about whether what he believes is rational, as long as it "feels" right to him. We cannot approach the postmodern generation with clever arguments of reason and logic. You have to speak to us in our own language. Gen X'ers value feelings and relationships, not dispassionate knowledge and logical arguments.

Don't be alarmed by this view of reality. Absolute truth does exist, but it is irrelevant until it becomes relative to me. Jesus said, "You shall know the truth, and the truth shall make you free." (John 8:32) Freedom is in knowing the truth. When you know the truth personally, that is relative (relational) truth. If the postmodern person is seeking to develop their own sense of reality, Jesus, who is the Truth, can work with that. The absolute becomes relative. When we stand before the Lord, it's not what we know that matters, but who we know. The intimate knowledge of Christ is the final and most satisfying destination of the postmodern journey.

2. Our hunger causes us to wander in search of something more authentic and spiritual.

Although the postmodern mindset represents a temporary abandonment of the rationalist belief system, it does allow for the existence of realities that science cannot measure, such as the supernatural, the spiritual, and the eternal. Gen X'ers are into "spirituality" but very skeptical of religious institutions. Many of them are more open to finding God outside the walls of organized "Christian" religion. They are attracted to New Age, Satanism, occult, crystals, aliens, psychic phenomena, pagan religions, and the like. As they have observed their parents' pursuit of material things, they seem to know that the answers they seek are to be found in the spiritual part of life. They just do not know where to look.

They believe that we, as a human race, have tried Christianity and Jesus, and it hasn't worked. Often the term "postmodern" is replaced synonymously with "post-Christian." Many believe that the Christian era has come to an end and a New Age has begun. People in my generation think they know what Jesus is all about. They therefore do not even bother to investigate Him as an option. They have a non-traditional approach to spirituality, which often comes across as being very irreverent.

Perhaps they are right. Maybe Christendom is coming to an end.

Is it possible that God too is interested in burying "Christianity" as we know it? Generation X is making a distinction between spirituality and religion. Maybe it's time for the church to make this same distinction. Is it possible that Jesus has been misrepresented through Christian organizations and institutions? G.K. Chesterton said, "Christianity hasn't been tried and found wanting; it has been found hard and left untried." This describes the great discrepancy between Jesus' example and the condition of church in the West.

People also tend to not trust the clergy as they once did. We have read too many newspaper articles with horrifying stories of child abuse and secret sins. Most people you talk to on the street would condemn TV evangelists to the category of "despicable," along with the drug dealer and organized crime boss. Many in my generation do not place any faith in the heart of organized religion or the papal system. I have a friend in his mid-twenties, who has spent the last several years trying to undo the devastation in his life caused by the sexual abuse he endured from a trusted church leader. I know another young lady who hasn't connected with a body of believers in years, for fear of condemnation. She has felt the sting of judgment from "church people" many times, for the way she dressed and how she expressed her artistic nature. It was reminiscent of a modern day witch-hunt. Everyone has his or her story. It's all too familiar. We live in a generation that feels the clergy cannot be trusted. We have stumbled and are not too willing to get back up again.

I have pleaded with Gen X seekers that if they were serious about their quest for something spiritual in their life, they should give Jesus a thorough investigation. His life, teaching, death and resurrection has had too great of an impact on the world to simply overlook Him in our spiritual journey. I invite them to meet with me for coffee, or in small groups in a home, and discover the real Jesus. They can ask any question they want. They can wrestle through the issues in the context of mutual dialogue and relationship. This is something that could never happen in a Sunday morning church service. This is the organic church. Jesus must be represented outside the walls and in the world where people live.

I find that most of the postmodern people I know who aren't even settled on Jesus yet, are completely open to getting prayer and being touched in their emotions. Remember that they are seeking for a spiritual encounter and authentic experience with God. There was one night in particular that a few of us were meeting in my home. One young lady who was in her early twenties was earnestly checking Jesus out. I asked if I could pray for her. Early into the prayer she began to weep, as the Holy Spirit ministered His love to her. After this she realized that her entire body was frozen to the seat she was sitting on. She couldn't move a muscle for more than twenty minutes. She identified it as God's presence being too overwhelming for her physical body. This experience profoundly impacted her in her journey to knowing God.

3. There are so many other possibilities.

Gen Xers have embraced the postmodern idea that truth is relative, and therefore they have become "pluralists" at heart. Our culture includes the worship of many gods and there are as many paths as there are individuals. They believe that everyone is worshipping the same God in different ways. They value and uphold all religions as legitimate and truth for those that follow them. "Just don't push your religion on me!"

The end result of pluralism is indecision. When there is an increase in the number of options, the ability to make a decision decreases. Have you ever been at a restaurant that has every meal known to man on its menu? I find it very difficult to decide what to have. What I tend to do is just order the same thing I always have…chicken. Ordering something new is always risky. What if it doesn't taste as good as they describe it?

I have observed four primary ways people cope with the many choices there are in regards to God and spirituality. The first is what I already alluded to. "I will just go with what I have always known." This option weighs heavy on reliance upon tradition. "I was born Anglican, and I will die an Anglican." People who have chosen this method of operating are very difficult to convince otherwise, because of their allegiance to that particular worldview inherited from their parents. Postmodernism has given this new generation courage to search outside the parameters that the individual has been raised to follow.

Another way to respond to the invasion of multiple religious paths is to simply believe that we cannot know which path is true. This position would maintain that it is impossible to know who God is and what He wants, if He even wants anything from us at all. This would typically be called "agnostic." If we can't know, then we are let off the hook. We can breathe again. We don't have to make a choice. Perhaps this isn't as bad as it looks. Maybe what the agnostic or atheist is really saying is, "I don't buy into the version of God that you're trying to sell me."

The third and most popular response is believing that everything is God and all religions are from Him. They assert the idea that all religions are basically the same, teaching the same messages about loving fellow man and working to attain some spiritual state of enlightenment.

This is easy. There is no wrong answer. You can't lose. The choice has been reduced to no choice at all. It's just a matter of preference.

However, the most "dangerous" and the fourth response to our pluralistic society is believing that there is one correct path and that we all must follow it. What a risk this is! What if out of all the choices there is only one that works? People can't handle that. This idea demands too much from us—a much more difficult road than the other three. The other options eliminate the risk and allow us to do what we want.

In this way, there are only really two options, yes or no, on or off, one or zero. Maybe this is what this generation is longing for. In the midst of all this confusion, they need to hear something simple; something different than what is being taught by the culture. On one hand there is Jesus and on the other there is everything else.

Jesus must be our message once again. The religion of "Christianity" is not much different than any other religion. The world doesn't need to hear about our church or denomination. Everything is Jesus and He is everything. Pluralism is providing God's people a backdrop to accentuate how glorious and unique Christ is. The light of a candle shines brighter in the midst of complete darkness.

4. We fear assimilation.

Are you a "Trekkie"? You know, "to boldly go where no man has gone before." I am a huge fan of the sci-fi television show *Star Trek: The Next Generation*. I have gained much insight into our culture by watching this show. It's interesting to notice how the original series with Captain Kirk and Spock reflect the values of modernism. *Next Generation* is "postmodern" all the way.

In *Next Generation* the greatest threat to the Federation, Captain

Jean Luc Picard, and his starship, is a diabolical race called "The Borg." The members of this alien army are half-biological and half-mechanical. They travel through the galaxy encountering diverse civilizations and societies, assimilating their citizens into their own single collective mind. They insert microscopic nano-probes into your blood stream that travel around infecting your DNA, slowly transforming you into one of them. They are ugly.

The worst thing about The Borg is that there is no individuality at all. Every unit is connected to the whole, and there is no capacity for individual thought or expression. This is feared most in a postmodern universe. Their infamous greeting of any species they happen to cross paths with is *"We are Borg...you will be assimilated...resistance is futile."*

Many young people today have similar feelings about organized church. They look at the institutional church as The Borg. They are afraid of an environment that is controlling, restricting, and mass-producing individuals that all look and act the same.

This generation embraces diversity. We love differences, and yet we're united. Being together while still retaining our individual identity is important. We despise being forced into a mold. We are comfortable appreciating diverse music styles, fashions, and self-expressions like tattooing and body piercing. There exists a fierce demand for individual freedom and rights in this postmodern generation. We dream of a church that would receive us the way we are, without attempting to assimilate us into the status quo.

THE EMERGING CHURCH

A close friend of mine often says, "Where you are—that is where

God has you." He is referring to the sovereignty of God. God is able to use what is happening in your life to fashion and move you toward His purpose. This is the lesson of Joseph's life. Even negative experiences or personal failure are all part of God's process in bringing us toward the destination. We must understand that the social hardships and cultural shifts being experienced by this generation are still under the control of the Sovereign God. However difficult it may be to receive, the world (Egypt) has become a place of preparation and protection. In this way, the emerging generation is not quite emerging yet. We are still hiding.

People talk about the "emerging church." They refer to new expressions of church that are geared towards reaching the postmodern generations. However, I don't see any evidence that there is an emerging church. The few examples of churches that are being labeled "emerging" seem to be a new version of a "seeker-friendly" model of church aimed at reaching postmoderns. However, the basic old form of church is intact. They usually just serve better coffee, sit on couches instead of pews, have more 'hang-out' time, and play more relevant music. I don't think the time to build is at hand. It is a season of deconstruction. The emerging church is yet to be seen.

The remainder of this book takes a prophetic look at what I believe things will look like in the not so distant future. We are going on a journey back in history to the time of David, Daniel, and to what Jesus started over two thousand years ago, giving us a foretaste of what I believe He is doing in this generation. It is my desire that God uses some of these insights to help you embrace the great change coming over the church, and that it would create in you a desire to experience the things you're about to see.

Emerging (Or Hidden) Generation?

NOTES:

1. Using AGI (Alan Guttmacher Institute) figures through 2002, estimating 1,293,000 abortions for 2003-05, and factoring in the possible 3% undercount AGI estimates for its own figures, the total number of abortions performed in the U.S. since 1973 equals 47,282,923. www.nrlc.org/abortion/facts/abortionstats.html.

CHAPTER SIX

GOD MAKES HOUSE CALLS

Nothing is ever really new. What is happening has happened before. What God is doing in a massive way around the world, He has done in other generations and at other times in history. Much of that history is contained in the pages of Scripture. Understanding our times means looking back into the past at seasons similar to our own. What was God doing in those days? Why was He doing them? What were the lessons to be learned? Everything we need to be able to gain understanding about our own present day situation is found in the stories and experiences recorded in the Scriptures.

My purpose in writing this book is to give insight into the church's current situation by looking at what God has already shown us about His ways. We have now come to a crucial moment in this journey together. I've told my story. I've described a need to change since new wine must be poured into new wineskins. We've examined God's master plan that I call the "apostolic dream" and how God has uniquely equipped the postmodern generation, somehow immune to religiosity, to carry these changes into the future. Now we turn our attention to God's perspective. I believe He is the initiator and the one driving this worldwide shift. What is the Holy Spirit up to? *Why* has Jesus left the building? To answer these questions, once again, we must go back. I want to tell you three stories, one wrapped in another, wrapped in yet another.

THE FIRST CHURCH CONFERENCE

We find the first of the three stories in the fifteenth chapter of Acts. Before Jesus ascended to the Father He commanded His followers to wait in Jerusalem for the promise of the Holy Spirit. When this happened, Jesus told them they would be empowered from heaven to be His witnesses. He gave them the plan of their missionary advancement, starting in Jerusalem and going out to the ends of the earth. This was a clear map for the apostles and the early church to follow. They were to start in one place and go out from there. It was quite simple. Yet not long into it, the spread of the gospel hit a wall.

In an earlier chapter I wrote about how often we don't really understand what God is saying to us because of the "grid" in our minds. We don't think like God does, and the minute we perceive what He is saying we change it in our minds according to our experiences and worldview. This is precisely what was going on at this point in the life of the earliest church. The purity of the gospel message and its advancement was now in danger of becoming shipwrecked by a Jewish mindset rooted in religious tradition. The first believers were all Jews. They knew that the gospel would spread to Gentile regions, but they obviously understood this to mean something different than what God had intended.

Some of the believers in Jerusalem had a problem with the work that Paul was doing with non-Jews. Even though they had this word from Jesus Himself, when it actually began to happen they were offended by it. It was troubling to them that Paul preached the gospel to the Gentiles without requiring them to embrace Jewish law and culture. Paul and his company were allowing Gentiles to enter into relationship with Christ without instructing them to convert to Judaism first. Even though these early Jewish disciples of Jesus knew the Gentiles were going to be a part of this, the whole idea of Gentiles being included in God's plan took a form they didn't expect.

Apparently the church in Jerusalem initially assumed that the Gentiles would be obligated to uphold their Jewish traditions. These men and women did not even think for a moment that God would abandon that tradition altogether. In their mind, it was clear that God had made His home with Israel. They were "in" and everyone else was "out." Therefore, in order for a Gentile to come to faith, that Gentile would first become Jewish and then Christian. Specifically this conversion would be symbolized by the physical act of circumcision required by the Law of Moses.

In our Western grid of "church," we too are requiring unbelievers to first embrace our religious culture to find Christ. Church comes first, and Christ is second. We are demanding the unbeliever to first sort through the foreign language and experience of our "Christian culture," in hopes that they meet Jesus somewhere in the mess of it all. We are inviting the world to church instead of to relationship with God, through Christ. We have expectations of new believers to quickly learn "our ways." We might as well be circumcising them. In effect, we are acting like the "false brothers" that Paul referred to in his letter to the Galatians. I spend more time undoing the damage that false Christianity has done to the seekers I have relationship with than I care to admit.

This generation is more apt to look at Jesus if He is standing alone. If you put "church" into the equation, you've lost them. Can you blame them? Don't you think that God could abandon the form that "church" presently takes in order to open the doors for others to find Jesus? This is exactly what the Lord did in Paul's day with the "Jewish Christian culture." Churchgoers may not even consider the possibility that God would want to change things. Too often our idea of all that God is able to do is confined to this tiny box, limiting God to "church." We have this sort of paradigm, just the same as the early Jewish believers did.

Many are praying for and believing that a harvest of souls is coming. We think that when this begins to happen, unbelievers are going to be lining up at our buildings, and we'll need to resort to holding multiple church services. The public will have to arrive at 6 a.m. to be able to find a seat at our 10 a.m. Sunday gathering. We have no idea that when this move of the Spirit actually begins to break out it's not going to look anything like that. They don't want to come to our churches, and I don't think they should have to. I don't think it is the heart of God to have our religious systems imposed on them. This is what Acts 15 is all about.

God was saving the Gentiles and meeting them outside the walls of the Jewish tradition. I believe that God is doing this again. Jesus is touching and leading people by His Spirit, outside the walls of organized church. There is going to be such a tension in all of this. It's going to be the same kind of tension we find in Acts. People are going to think this is unbiblical and completely out of order. "This cannot be God!" However, as you read these pages I hope that you begin to see that this is God!

Expectedly, most of the time given to consider the matter of the "Gentiles" was spent in debate and dispute. (Acts 15:6) It was all out war. They were getting nowhere really fast. Then all of a sudden, the tide turned.

Peter rose up and said to them, "Men and brethren, you know that a good while ago God chose among us that by my mouth the Gentiles should hear the word of the gospel and believe. So God, who knows the heart acknowledged them by giving them the Holy Spirit just as He did to us, and made no distinction between us and them, purifying their hearts by faith. Now therefore, why do you test God by putting a yoke on the neck of the disciples, which neither our fathers nor we were able to bear? But we believe that through the grace of the Lord Jesus Christ we shall be saved in the same manner as they." Then all the multitude kept silent and listened to Barnabas and Paul declaring how many miracles and wonders God had worked through them among the Gentiles. (Acts 15:7-12)

The Spirit of God was moving in the silence. The hearts of men were breaking. Old ways of thinking and misinterpretation of Scripture were melting away, as the church in Jerusalem heard story after story. It was undeniable. God was moving outside their way of thinking.

And after they had become silent, James answered saying, "Men and brethren, listen to me, Simon (Peter) has declared how God at first visited the Gentiles to take out of them a people for His name. And with this the words of the prophets agree, just as it is written: 'After this I will return and I will rebuild the tabernacle of David, which has fallen down; I will rebuild its ruins, and I will set it up; so that the rest of mankind may seek the Lord, Even all the Gentiles who are called by My name, says the Lord who does all these things." (Acts 15:13-17)

When James heard the story of how God used Simon Peter to first visit the Gentiles, James said, "This is Amos 9:11." This is the verse concerning the "rebuilding of the tabernacle of David." What in the world does the tabernacle of David have to do with this issue they're facing with the Gentiles in the book of Acts? What is the tabernacle of David? All we know at this point is that the penny dropped for James when he heard Peter tell his story. Therefore, whatever this "tabernacle of David" is, it has something to do with understanding the events surrounding Peter's first experience preaching to Gentiles. This brings us to the second story.

THE JOPPA EXPERIENCE

You can find the second story and all its details in Acts chapter ten. I am going to retell it here briefly. There were two people praying. One man was sitting on a roof of a house in a city called Joppa. The other man praying was a Roman centurion, about fifty miles away in Caesarea. Peter, who was in Joppa, knew Christ personally, as an apostle of our Lord. The other man was called Cornelius. He was serious about seeking God, but was considered to be an outsider to the commonwealth of Israel. Cornelius was a Gentile. He didn't know God, although he prayed to God and gave to the poor. He was seeking the truth. This is a beautiful story of how these two men came together by an unusual string of circumstances, arranged by God Himself. Let's start in Joppa.

It was about noon and Peter was terribly hungry. I believe that he was fasting. The rooftop was a place where Peter enjoyed relaxing and praying. However, this would be no ordinary day. Suddenly, Peter fell into a trance. This word in Greek is the verb *existemi*, of which we get the English word "ecstasy." Peter was awake and yet in some kind of euphoric dream state. It was as though what God was about to tell Peter must bypass the ordinary processes of the mind, in an elevated God-consciousness. God didn't want Peter's brain to get in the way of receiving the message. In this state, Peter saw a vision from heaven.

A massive sheet held by its four corners descended from heaven to earth. On this sheet Peter saw many ritually unclean animals of the earth, "wild beasts, creeping things, and birds of the air." These were animals that were forbidden for God's people to eat, according to the Law. As Peter looked upon this sight, he heard a powerful voice declare "Kill and eat!" Peter responded with religious conviction and fervor. He had the right "Sunday School" answer. "Not so, Lord, for I have never eaten anything common or unclean." The voice replied with this shocking statement, "What God has declared 'clean,' you must not call unclean." This happened three times, and the sheet was once again taken up into heaven.

Peter was completely perplexed by the vision. He was probably thinking, "What? Does God want me to eat pork now?" Peter had no clue what the vision meant. Often when God speaks to us, we really don't understand what He is saying. This is by design on God's part. He doesn't want us to go out on our own initiative to act on what was just heard. Many times we don't stick around to listen for further details. We are not supposed to do anything with what God has just revealed to us. He speaks something to us and our job is to wait. Don't do anything with that word, vision, or any other divine communication. Just wait. This word was not given to direct you, but to confirm something down the road. It is a signpost. When the time is right, you will understand the vision. Peter was very confused about what he had just witnessed.

He didn't get it!

Meanwhile over in Caesarea, the centurion, Cornelius, was having his own unusual experience in prayer. First of all, it is quite interesting that the Roman was praying at all. In fact, he not only prayed, but also gave alms to the poor. Isn't that amazing? Here's a guy who was searching for God, but had no idea who He was. Yet these are the two things his heart led him to do: to pray, and to give to the poor. I believe Cornelius symbolizes the many millions of people in our own culture who do not know God, but are praying.

In a recent survey reported by Reader's Digest (November 2003), 64% of Canadians say "Yes, definitely," they strongly believe in God. Another 14% say that they "somewhat believe" in God. Almost 8 in 10 people I see everyday, driving in their cars, or walking down the street, believe that God exists. These percentages are even higher in the United States. Yet only 23% of Canadians regularly attend a weekly worship service. Among those who do not attend church, spiritual pursuit is still a high value. 45% of Canadians claim to pray every day. Let's do the math. About 25 million Canadians (80%) believe in God, but only 7 million of them "go to church." However, over 14 million are praying. Assuming the people going to church are actually praying, there are at least 7 million people praying every day who don't attend religious services. To explain these trends, one Canadian told Reader's Digest, "God makes house calls."

In this story, Cornelius represents perhaps hundreds of millions of people praying outside the walls, right around the globe. Maybe there is more prayer going on in the world than in the church right now. It seems that people have a deep desire to connect with God, but they don't know who He is. I wonder what their prayers are like. More than anything, perhaps the cry of the culture is "Help!" It's a tumultuous world that we live in. People are more open to God now than ever before. They are calling on God and God will not ignore these prayers. They are literally ascending before Him. In response, the Lord sent an angel to Cornelius in a vision.

The angel appeared to Cornelius with a message. "Your prayers and your alms have come up as a memorial before God." The angel went on to instruct Cornelius to send for a man named Peter, over in Joppa. He gave him the address to his house and told Cornelius that Peter "would tell him what he must do."

Remember, Peter had just seen his three visions of the sheet, unclean animals, and "kill and eat." He didn't understand what God was saying, but suddenly there was a knock at the door. It was the men sent by Cornelius to escort Peter to his home. Before Peter realized who was at the door, the Holy Spirit said to him, "Behold, three men are seeking you. Arise therefore, go down and go with them, doubting nothing; for I have sent them. " (See Acts 10:19-20) Peter didn't realize who these men were or where he was being led. Peter was on a need-to-know basis with God. If he understood where he was being taken, he probably wouldn't have gone. As you can guess, Peter followed those men, bringing some of his Jewish Christian friends along. They were extremely shocked when they arrived at their destination.

Peter was set up. God brought him to a place he would never go. Cornelius had his whole house filled with friends and relatives, and they were all unbelieving Gentiles. Do you realize that it was forbidden for a Jewish person to even set foot in the house of a Gentile? They would never eat a meal with a Gentile. It was considered sinful to do so. If this situation had happened before his Joppa experience, it would have been a "no-brainer" for Peter. "We are not supposed to go to places like this. It is not proper for 'Christians' to hang out with people like that." These unbelievers were dirty. Yet I imagine the Holy Spirit whispering these words into the ear of Peter, at the "awful" sight of a house full of Gentiles: "Do not call unclean what I have called clean."

Suddenly it all made sense. The Holy Spirit wasn't talking about not eating pork! He was confronting Peter's prejudice and heart attitude against a people group. The vision back in Joppa was for this moment. It became a signpost telling Peter, "You are here." He was in the right place at the right time, even against his better judgment. God was doing something new, and Peter needed a radical shift in his perception. Peter now recognized that the Holy Spirit had set up this appointment. God was indeed making a "house call."

Peter entered the room and lifted up his voice in the crowded home saying, "You know how unlawful it is for a Jewish man to keep company with or go to one of another nation. But God has shown me that I should not call any man common or unclean." (Acts 10:28) As Peter shared the gospel with those people, many of them started believing the message. Before the ex-fisherman was finished speaking, the Holy Spirit was poured out on that first little band of Gentiles. They were all baptized that day. Peter and his Jewish friends marveled at what had happened. They couldn't believe their eyes. This was unprecedented. God was doing something they had never seen or even imagined.

The Lord is saying this very thing right now to the church. "Don't call them unclean. I'm changing your grid. I'm changing how you are to understand this thing. I'm not requiring them to embrace your religious culture to meet me. I'm going to meet them where they're at. I'm going over to their house to bring my love to them."

This is the story James heard in the conference of Acts 15. This story would be a partial fulfillment of something spoken by the prophet Amos, generations before. James said, "This is Amos 9:11." The story of Peter and Cornelius is all about God rebuilding the tabernacle of David. We are getting closer to unveiling this powerful truth, but we need one more story. I believe that God is doing something in our times like He did in Acts 10 and 15. However, it goes back even further. We must now go back one thousand years before Peter and Cornelius. It is with David that this picture comes into clearer focus.

DAVID'S TABERNACLE

Part of this third story has already been told in chapter four. When the ark of the covenant was captured by the Philistines, after causing them much trouble, it was sent back to the land of Israel on a cart. The cart was tied to two cows. The cows left their young calves behind and pulled the cart without a yoke. The Philistines watched as the cows took the straight path all the way to Bethshemesh, neither turning left nor right. It was so unnatural for these cows to leave their young. It was supernatural. God was leading the way. They brought the ark right to the house of Abinadab, where it stayed for many decades until David came to retrieve it.

The fact is, everyone knew it was there. You know how rumors spread. However, no one knew what to do with it. Finally, when David became king, God showed him where the ark truly belonged.

The logical answer to the question of "Where does the ark, the manifest presence of God, belong?" is "Put it back where it came from." Before the Philistines captured it, where did God live? If you remember, the ark traveled around the wilderness with Moses and his portable tabernacle. However, once Joshua and all his people conquered and settled the land of Canaan, the tabernacle of Moses, along with the ark of the covenant, found its home in a place called Shiloh. It remained there for several hundred years, until the ark was finally captured and taken to the land of the Philistines. The ark was considered to be the presence of God, so when it was taken, God was also taken. God was gone from the nation of Israel. God had been out of the loop for a long time. King David was the man to change that. However, he had something quite radical in mind.

I'm sure that most Israelites, especially the priests, assumed that David would place the ark back in the tabernacle of Moses, where it once was. The tabernacle of Moses was ready, all set up on Mount Gibeon. The priests were also ready to perform their duties and offer the daily sacrifices. Everything was in position except for the most important piece of all—the ark. Again, I play conversations in my head of what those around David might have said to him. "Alright, David, let's bring this back. Let's restore the proper order. Place the ark behind the veil, in the Most Holy Place. Let's get this set up again. We will burn the incense, perform the cleansing rituals and ceremonies, administer the burnt offerings and sin offerings, and restore proper biblical order. Return God to the tabernacle of Moses!"

David might have found such talk to be inspiring until he realized what this would entail. The tabernacle of Moses meant that one man in the whole nation could actually go into the Most Holy Place, where the ark would sit, and see God. Only the High Priest could do this. One man out of millions of people could meet with God; just one. Furthermore, the High Priest would only do this on one day of the year, the Day of Atonement. So here we have it: one man on one day was allowed to see God. This is the tabernacle of Moses. Somewhere in David's contemplation of the matter, a shift took place. David was not settled on returning the ark to the place it was before. Instinctively, he knew that God wasn't into that. The Lord was changing things, and it took much courage for David to do what he did next.

David must have gathered all the most influential people in the nation together. I envision the silence in the room when he delivered the news. "Guys, I've got different plans, actually. I'm not bringing the ark back to the tabernacle of Moses." What was David talking about? Was he about to change hundreds of years of tradition, as well as challenging the Mosaic Law itself? The tabernacle of Moses was set up by God! Much of the Mosaic Law centered on the activities of the tabernacle. The Most Holy Place is the only place the ark was to be. However, David had a different idea. Instead, he pitched a tent in his backyard and told his opposition, "The ark is coming home with me!"

As we saw in a previous chapter, David's first attempt to recover the ark ended in tragedy. David followed the footsteps of the Philistines and put the ark on a cart. God permitted the oxen to stumble. The Almighty didn't want to be carried that way. It was a hard lesson for David. In response David said, "How can the ark of the Lord come to me?" David's heart was revealed in this trial. All he wanted was God to come to him. He wanted God to himself, and now this was a huge hurdle in the way of David's dream being realized. Thankfully, David discovered what he did wrong and three months later they tried again.

David brought the ark out from the house of Obed-Edom, with praise, rejoicing, music, and dancing. Thousands of people lined the streets of the city as the procession continued, finally reaching Mount

Zion, David's house. The tent was there and the ark was brought to its new location. Never again would the tabernacle of Moses be inhabited by God. You could now find Him in a humble tent in the backyard of the king. (1 Chronicles 15, 16, 17)

The tabernacle of David was a place of continual prayer and worship. David set up singers and musicians to minister before the Lord twenty-four hours a day. Many of the psalms were written in that place. Powerful prophetic glimpses of future realities and the coming Messiah were seen in that tent. Simple songs became prophetic Scripture. For example, Psalm 22 accurately depicts the crucifixion of our Lord a thousand years before it happened and before "crucifixion" was even invented. David and his friends enjoyed countless hours with their God. It was a place of intimacy and love. The totally amazing thing about it was that David had to break half the Mosaic Law to actually pull this off. He did not restrict entrance or access to the ark.

If you were to tell Moses and Aaron and the Levites of the past that this would happen one day, they would say that it was impossible. The question would be asked, "Did these people who came before the ark drop dead?" As we know, the answer would be "No." God seemed to like this. He was in it. The Lord was the One behind the changes David made, even though it seemed improper. In David's tent, God could be with His people. There was no veil of separation. All could come before Him. David knew the times. The old was passing away, and something new and wonderful was emerging. I believe that the heart of David did not want to go back to the old system of worship, where some other guy got to meet with God. He wanted God to himself.

SOMETHING IS MISSING

For a period of about forty years, there were two tabernacles in operation. Although David had the ark to himself and his musician friends, he permitted the tabernacle of Moses to continue with its sacrifices and rituals. We have here two mountains, Mount Zion and Mount Gibeon. There were two tabernacles, but only one of them had God's presence. It's unimaginable to think that the priests carried on business-as-usual in the tabernacle of Moses. They shed the blood of animals, performed the cleansing rituals, baked the bread, lit the candles, and burned the incense. They were proper and customary, doing all things commanded by Moses in the Law, but one critical element was missing. The ark was not behind the veil of the Most Holy Place. God was not there.

Have you ever felt like you're just going through the motions, "going to church," and you walk away frustrated and empty? You may think to yourself, "Where was God today?" Now, don't get me wrong. God lives with you, and in every believer. There is nowhere in the world we can go where He is not there. However, I'm speaking of that very real sense that He is close and actively involved with His people. There is a growing hunger in our hearts for His presence to be clearly manifest among us. Instead, we often come away from church with a nagging awareness that something is missing.

GOD LEAVES THE BUILDING

Asaph was a key worship leader in the tabernacle of David, and one of David's friends. He wrote several psalms, presumably while ministering before the Lord in David's tent. Psalm 78 was written by Asaph and it speaks of Israel's history from eternity's perspective. Psalm 78 is a divine commentary on the last several hundred years preceding the time of David. Most of the theme of this very long song reflects Israel's unfaithfulness to God and His reaction to their idolatry.

Yet they tested and provoked the Most High God, and did not keep His testimonies, but turned back and acted unfaithfully like their fathers; they were turned aside like a deceitful bow. For they provoked Him to anger with their high places, and moved Him to jealousy with their carved images. When God heard this, He was furious, and greatly abhorred Israel, so that He forsook the tabernacle of Shiloh, the tent He had placed among men, and delivered His strength into captivity, and His glory into the enemy's hands. He also gave His people over to the sword, and was furious with His inheritance. The fire consumed their young men; and their maidens were not given in marriage. Their priests fell by the sword, and their widows made no lamentation. Then the Lord awoke as from sleep, like a mighty man who shouts because of wine. And He beat back His enemies; He put them to a perpetual reproach. Moreover He rejected the tent of Joseph, and did not choose the tribe of Ephraim; but chose the tribe of Judah, Mount Zion which He loved. And He built His sanctuary like the heights, like the earth which He has established forever. (Psalm 78:56-69)

Just imagine how shocking this song would have been to the people listening to Asaph, as he sang this prophetic revelation. The Philistines did not steal God by capturing the ark. God walked out! God actually purposefully walked out of the tabernacle of Moses and let himself be captured by the Philistines for a short season. They didn't take God. God left the building. He delivered His strength and glory into the hands of His enemies. He was waiting for the right time and the right person who would do what He wanted to be done. God's plan was to set up shop somewhere else. He was breaking all the rules. God loved Mount Zion. It wasn't sufficient for God either, to meet with one man on one day a year. He always had it in His heart to enjoy fellowship with all people. This is what the tabernacle of David represents, intimacy with God.

There were no animals slain in David's tent. There was no veil separating God from His people. Anyone could come in before His presence and meet with the Living God. David walked in a position with God that wouldn't be fully realized for a thousand years. The tabernacle of David foreshadows the time of the new covenant, where each believer in Christ has full access to the Most Holy Place. God has removed the barriers to intimacy with Him. This is why He loved this tabernacle. This not only reflects the truth of the new covenant, but also prophesies the final destiny of the church and planet earth. Of all that God has done in the past, this is what He chose to rebuild once again. He really likes this one. "I'm going to do that one again. I'm going to rebuild the tabernacle of David."

How does this relate to Cornelius? Remember, James said that the Cornelius story is all about the fulfillment of the "rebuilding of David's tabernacle." God left the religious tradition of the Jews. He walked out, and was found at the house of a Gentile man. God put up His tent in Cornelius' backyard. Cornelius did not have to jump through all the hoops. Not only did God visit this man, He also met with his friends and family. The old covenant was like the tabernacle of Moses—the believers of Jerusalem wanted to keep God in the box of what they had always known. However, God was going out. The Holy Spirit wanted to go out into the real world and set up a tent in the backyard of whoever had a heart like David's. "How can the ark of God come to me?"

Jesus wants to meet every person in the place where they live. So when James heard this story of Cornelius, he said, "This is the tabernacle of David." I believe that God is rebuilding this tabernacle now in our day. God is working outside the walls of everything we've known. Are we going to be able to adjust and go with God on this one? It seems to me that God has no sacred cows. He's quite content to forsake what He has instituted in the past for something better or more fitting to His purpose. If only we were as flexible as He. We need His grace to help us change. The good news is that God does make house calls.

CHAPTER SEVEN

INVASION

I shouldn't be surprised that my journey has brought me to this point. I've come full circle, back to where I began. The very reason that I am a Christian today is because God made a house call on my family over twenty years ago. My first church was my dad, mom, and sister. Often we are able to predict where we may end up by noticing the signs embedded in the events of how we began. The future can be seen in every new birth.

I remember the early season of my life when God seemed so distant. Even as a child I would think about God, believing that God existed, but never knowing anything of Him. If someone were to ask me, I would have said I was "Catholic." "I am Portuguese, therefore I am Catholic." This is what my parents taught me. However, I don't ever remember going to Mass, not even on Christmas Eve or Easter. We must have been "bad" Catholics. This would explain why I had no idea what God was like. I didn't know that Jesus rose from the dead. No one ever told me that Jesus will return one day. The only time I ever prayed as a child was when I knew I was in trouble and that my father was going to spank me. "God if you're out there, please save me..." (I don't recall one instance where God answered these prayers.)

I don't have many memories of my childhood. In my mind's eye, a shadow was cast upon those early years of my development. What I remember most is how unhappy my parents were. My father always seemed angry and I was continually frightened of the moment he would explode. I found it difficult to ask him for anything. My mother was depressed and oppressed. Life was a heavy burden that only lifted when she slept.

My mother was also ill. For over three years she woke every morning with nausea and symptoms of the flu. She visited various doctors and specialists, but couldn't find anyone who could confirm that what she was experiencing had a definite medical explanation. They told her it was psychosomatic. It was "all in her head," and no one could help her. She was gripped by fear. She was afraid to leave the house. She felt unsafe. By the time I was twelve years old my parents were contemplating divorce. They were completely unhappy. Then it happened. None of us would have ever thought it was possible.

It was December in 1983. Mom was racing through the channels of the television, recuperating from her customary bout of morning sickness. All at once, the flicker of stations stopped at a program she had never seen before; it was a local talk show. The guest on the show was telling her story. My mother was instantly captured. The next few moments would prove to be the most important of her life. The woman spoke of her experience with people she encountered in her line of work as a psychiatric nurse. She had come to the conclusion that many sicknesses had their roots in emotional and spiritual darkness. My mother could relate to many of the things this woman said. She continued to testify about how she had seen God heal and set individuals free from the oppression in their lives. She accredited this miraculous experience to Jesus and spoke of Him with passion and deep love.

It was as though this woman actually knew Him. God was real to her and He really cared. My mother cried and God came near in the living room that day. God revealed Himself to her and she believed in Jesus. She always knew about Him, but had now, in a very real sense, finally met Him. She was saved in every way.

Over the next few months, Mom came to a place where she would jump out of bed and engage in her regular morning routine, but with one obvious difference. She wasn't sick. God had healed her. Joy began to seep through the cracks of her broken life and into the heart of a woman made free. She changed. She was not the same mom moping around the house. Something animated her once lifeless existence. Her fears melted like wax.

"What has gotten into Mom?" I had recently seen the remake of the 1956 science fiction thriller, *Invasion of the Body Snatchers.* That movie spooked me out. I was convinced that my mother's body had been taken over by extra-terrestrials. She seemed a little weird to me. Every free moment for her became an opportunity to pray and read the Bible. Then she did the unthinkable. She threw out my Michael Jackson *Thriller* album without asking my permission. When later questioned, to provide an adequate explanation for her madness, she indicated that the album "gave her the creeps." I was very upset over her actions; I admit that I was a huge fan. I wore the little white glove and was the first one to do the moonwalk in my junior high school. Maybe *I* was the one possessed by an alien.

Dad did not respond positively to the new changes. My father thought she was losing her mind. He couldn't understand how all of a sudden she had "found religion." He didn't like it at all. So he decided to fix things. He planned to do what he always did to get his way with her. All he would have to do is put a little pressure on her and she would renounce this newfound faith.

One day my father cornered Mom and announced that he was not going to tolerate this religious fanaticism under his roof. She had to make a decision. "It's me or Jesus! I am not going to stay with you if you are going to be like this," he warned. He must have thought she would submit to his ultimatum and deny her faith. My Dad did not know what he was up against. Her response was somewhat of a shock. She reaffirmed her love for him. Then she proceeded to say, "I would hate to see you leave, but I cannot deny Jesus. He healed me and saved my life. I love you but I love Jesus more." This rocked Dad's world. He ran out of the house. He needed some time to figure things out. What was happening? Was this real? Was this really God and where did that leave him? This was the beginning of the end of life as Dad knew it. He too would soon encounter this Being from another world.

My father started picking up the Bible behind Mom's back just to see what was getting into her. As he read the Scriptures, his heart softened and the light of the Gospel began to penetrate the darkness and deception he lived in. Then one night, only a few months after Mom's miraculous conversion, something wonderful happened. He woke up from a dream in the middle of the night, never feeling more frightened in his life. He shook Mom out of her sleep, in desperation, repeating over and over again, "I need your Jesus." She held him like a mother holding her newborn baby. He wept. He repented. Jesus saved him that night.

It didn't take me long to see what had occurred. My father's life took a drastic turn and I couldn't believe what was happening to my parents. Now Dad was praying, reading the Scriptures, and crying a lot. Tears were constantly flowing down his face as God initiated the process of healing him of the pain that was the source of his anger for so many years. *Oh no! They got Dad.* The invasion was unstoppable. I soon realized that something extra-dimensional was happening. It wasn't little green men from a distant planet millions of light years away. It was another dimension. The kingdom of God took root and was growing in our family. My parents passed from darkness to light, from death to life, and from the power of Satan to the power of God. However, the invasion was not complete.

My father's conversion had a significant impact on me. He shared his early experiences of Jesus with me. I remember one evening as I lay awake in bed thinking on the things taking place in our home, my father called up to me, "Paul, come downstairs, quick!" I thought something was wrong and I flew down the stairs to see what had transpired. When I entered the room, I was amazed at what I saw and heard. My father was sitting on the couch, with his hands lifted, and a Bible resting in his lap. Tears were streaming down his cheeks and he was speaking a language that I had never heard before.

"Dad, what is that?" I asked. He told me of how he was reading in the first few chapters of the book of Acts in the Bible. It chronicles the account of early believers being filled with the Holy Spirit and how, as a result, they spoke in "other tongues." It was a language they did not learn; yet God gave them the ability to speak it for the purpose of magnifying Him. My father, in child-like faith, simply asked God if he could receive a blessing like this. I stood in awe and wonder as he said, "So I started speaking in tongues, just like the ones here in Acts." I was truly happy for Dad. God had become the Father that he never had. I went up to my room with a smile on my face. The next day I told all my friends at school, "My dad speaks in tongues." No one knew what it was, so I had to explain it. All day peers were coming up to me asking about it. I don't know what made me tell all my schoolmates. I guess I was truly excited that God was visiting my home. The reality of God had met me face to face.

One afternoon, in the spring of 1984, my mother and I sat down together in the living room and she explained to me all that had happened to Dad and her. She shared with me the message of Christ and of the cross that He carried for me. I was twelve years old. I still had never been in a "church service." I had never heard the choir singing the old hymn "Just As I Am", nor felt the tug of the preacher calling me to come to the altar. It was a simple conversation with Mom and no external prompting to incite an emotional response. The gospel was spoken to me and I believed. I remember feeling the weight of my sin and the joy of being forgiven. Even though I was young, I knew I needed to be saved. It pleased God to reveal His Son to me in that moment and it changed my life forever.

Over the following summer months, my home and my family experienced the habitation of God. Each night we engaged in a simple routine following the supper meal. After cleaning up, my parents would put my little sister to bed and then gather with me in the living room. Every night was as though we walked right into the tabernacle of David. We met with God. My father had started learning to play the acoustic guitar, but at this point he only knew two chords, A minor and E minor. So that is what he played. He moved back and forth between the two chords, with slight delays as he worked at placing his fingers to produce a clear sound. Dad, Mom, and I would sing to this A minor and E minor sound. We would sing for hours. Often we didn't go to bed until after midnight. We didn't know the latest worship choruses. We didn't know any hymns. We would sing whatever was on our hearts, each one singing a different melody. It was so pure and passionate. Many times, all of us would be weeping as we experienced a depth of intimacy that I have only felt on a few occasions. This was the very first church that I had ever been a part of. Little did I know, it would sow the seed of discontent for anything less. Church would never be that good again.

CHAPTER EIGHT

THE CHURCH THAT JESUS STARTED

EXTREME MAKEOVER: CHURCH EDITION

Every Sunday night, millions tune in: "Put together one very run-down house, a deserving family, several opinionated designers, seven days and what do you get?" The answer is *Extreme Makeover: Home Edition.* Each episode of this highly successful reality program features a race against time on a project that would ordinarily take at least four months to achieve. It involves a team of designers, contractors and several hundred workers who have just seven days to totally rebuild an entire house—every single room, plus the exterior and landscaping. The lives of the lucky families are forever changed when they learn that they have been selected to have their home walls moved, their floors replaced and even their façades radically changed. Completely rebuilding a home in just seven days sounds quite familiar.

It took God the same amount of time to completely renew planet earth in Genesis, chapter one, from a chaotic formless mess to the beauty we see today. However, that project may not compare to the task of what Jesus is building these days.

Jesus told His disciples, "In my Father's house are many mansions; if it were not so, I would have told you. I go to prepare a place for you." (John 14:2) We know that His construction project is the church (See

Matthew 16:18), a cosmic "extreme makeover." Taking the church from what it is now and making it God's dream home is no small ambition.

Speaking of "church," my wife and I tried to go to church a few times after resigning from my pastoral position. Surprisingly, it took everything in us to get our bodies out of bed on Sunday mornings. We had started making the shift. Church was changing for us. Our best times were when our gang of friends would come over and fellowship together. I didn't know it then, but we were beginning to experience the rebuilding of the tabernacle of David. God was making a house call, just in time.

More and more I felt God leading us to be part of a church that met in houses, or coffee shops, or anywhere outside the walls of the conventional church. The meeting place was really not the point. The point was that we wanted to be the church, out in the world. The building was fading behind us in the distance. There was no turning back.

One day as I was meditating on what the church should look like, I asked the Lord to give me a picture from the Scriptures of the kind of church that He wanted. Although we entered a period of "detoxifying" where we abstained from predictable church activity, I knew that we couldn't stay there forever. God would lead us into a new expression of church. I was leery of throwing the baby out with the bathwater. What were we to keep from our past church experience? What should we throw out? And, what did God want to redefine for us? Therefore, I asked the Lord for something visual and simple. I asked God to give me a blueprint that we could follow and use as a standard to keep us in line with His heart.

WE WERE NEVER TOLD TO PLANT CHURCHES

I scoured through the first two chapters of Acts looking for principles and guidelines to planting a healthy church. What I learned later was that I was already beginning on the wrong foot. I had to unlearn something that was drilled into my head for many years. Did Jesus ever commission His disciples to plant churches? Although this is common practice and assumed to be an appropriate focus, planting churches is not our primary mission. Let me explain.

The same day in May that God spoke to me about the apostolic dream, He also told me that my message was not to be "the church," but that my message was Jesus. I thought to myself, "Yeah, and…" There was nothing more to it. I mean, of course Jesus is the message. I didn't realize how misled I was until the next day.

I was pulling up to my house at the end of the day, and I saw a man putting a leaflet in my mailbox. As I got out of the car and approached the house, we met halfway down the sidewalk. I soon discovered that this man was a minister who had just moved to the neighborhood to plant a church. We had a great talk. He was going door to door handing out leaflets inviting people to the new church.

When I got into the house, I quickly read through the pamphlet. I loved it. I thought to myself, "This is something I would do." The write-up listed several reasons why people don't go to church today. Some of them were: "the music is outdated," "the sermons are boring and irrelevant," and the "people are cold and unfriendly." The new pastor assured people that it would not be so at his church. The leaflets continued to describe how contemporary the music would be, and how the messages were interesting and practical.

"This is what I was talking about yesterday," I thought. But then, the Holy Spirit showed me that the message was not Jesus. The message in this brochure was all about "the church." The goal was to plant a church. The objective was to get people into "church." Basically, it was saying, "This is why our church is better than all the others you've tried."

Now, again, I do not doubt the motives. Remember, I loved it. This is how I was trained. The idea is to get people in church so they can hear the gospel and come to faith in Christ. The problem is that the message of "church" gets in first before Jesus. This is built right into the foundation of these new potential converts. What may happen is that we produce *church-ians* instead of Christians.

Jesus was constantly on the lips of the early church. Their mission was given to them by Christ Himself. He used language like "go," "preach the gospel," "make disciples," and "be my witnesses." (See Mark 16:15-18; Matthew 28:18-20; Acts 1:8) There are a dozen times in the book of Acts where the phrase "preached Christ" is used, describing the mission and message of the first church. Jesus never told the apostles to plant churches. Churches resulted from preaching Christ. In a sense, they were planted by accident. They were a product of the great commission going forth. The apostles did not plant churches to win people to Christ. They made disciples; and churches were birthed out of that prime directive.

YOU'RE STARTING TOO LATE

Having said all this, at that time I was still in "church planting" mode. I defined myself as a church planter. I was going to unlock the mystery of the church in Acts. I was certain I could find the keys in Acts 1 and 2. Not far into my study I heard the unmistakable voice of the Holy Spirit whisper ever so softly as a thought into my mind: "You are starting too late!" I jolted to a stop. Then I heard, "This church started three years before Acts 1 and 2."

How intriguing this was to me. I had not really thought about it that way. Jesus "planted" the first church! The church in Acts 1 & 2 was birthed out of Jesus' time with His disciples. He laid the foundation of that church. When He said that He would "build His church" (Matthew 16:18), Jesus was actually doing that, as recorded in the gospels. I was starting to look at this too late in the game. I would need to turn to the gospels to see what Jesus' church looked like.

Most of us who have spent any time in and around the evangelical church have somehow inherited a "mental block" when it comes to Jesus. We read the gospels like history, but with no expectation that any of it actually applies to us today. You can see this barrier clearly when considering the things that Jesus did and taught.

There are many Christians who believe that the miracles and works of Jesus cannot be seen today. This notion is openly taught. The proponents of this school of thought claim that Jesus did what He did out of His divinity, and since none of us can rightly claim to be God we cannot access the miraculous as Jesus did. They maintain that the apostles of Acts were an exception to this rule for the purpose of establishing Christianity. However, they assert that now that the apostles are dead, miracles are dead too.

How then would you explain that all over the earth believers are moving in similar kinds of miracles as those we read about Jesus doing in the gospels? I've seen them myself. I believe that Jesus laid down the power He had from divinity when He became a man, and as a man did what He did depending on the Holy Spirit; as we also do now.

Then there are the teachings of Christ. Most, if not all, of Jesus' teachings were about the kingdom of God. I find that many Christians don't really understand what the kingdom of God is. The answer I hear most is "It is heaven" or "It's coming in the future, when Jesus returns." This is based on a teaching that basically upholds the idea that when the Jews rejected Christ's first advent, Jesus took the kingdom of God back up to heaven with Him. So instead of the kingdom, He gave us the "church age."

This is why we tend to hear more teaching out of the epistles of the New Testament than the words of Jesus. If the kingdom is up there somewhere or coming only in the future, then most of Jesus' teaching is irrelevant to us. Yet part of the great commission is to teach disciples to obey everything Jesus commanded. How many new disciples are truly rooted in Jesus' teaching of the kingdom, I wonder?

So there you have it, a mental block about Jesus. We can't do what He did and we can't live what He taught. So what's the point? This kind of blindness to Jesus also affects our understanding of church. What is the modern understanding of church based on? At best, Christians would probably say, "The epistles of Paul." However, most of what the epistles describe as "church" doesn't really connect with what we know church to be. For example, how does this work: "Whenever you come together, each of you has a psalm, has a teaching, has a tongue, has a revelation, and has an interpretation." (1 Corinthians 14:26) How could you possibly do this at church on Sunday? Everyone bring something to the meeting? The service would go on for hours, and yet not everyone would have their opportunity to share.

Even the instructions in the epistles are based on an understanding and foundation laid before the epistles were ever written. Jesus laid the foundation in the hearts and experiences of twelve men and the wider community we see in the gospel writings. Jesus is the one who took the common Greek word *ecclesia*, which meant "ones called out," and redefined it for His purpose. This is the word that translates "church" and it was first introduced to us by Jesus in Matthew 16:18. He declared that He "will build His church and the gates of Hades shall not prevail against it." Jesus was building His church right there, in His earthly ministry. Our model of church should be Jesus and the community that He led. If He is not the basis of what we call "church," then what are our traditional ideas of church based on?

When we say the word "church," a familiar picture comes to mind of a large gathering of people, on Sundays, filling a chapel or temple, lining up in rows. At the altar stands a pastor or priest who speaks to his congregation. This concept would have seemed very strange to the early church. At that time the church primarily met in small clusters in a private house or the inner court of a private estate. Truly, the meeting space of the early church was not a cathedral, but a living room. In fact, the earliest Christians did not build any sanctuaries at all and met in homes for the first 250 years.

Then it happened in AD 312. The Roman Emperor Constantine converted to Christianity, and made it the religion of the state in his Edict of Milan. Christians, tired of centuries of hardship and persecution, celebrated Constantine as a "savior." Christians could now relax, but it came at a high price. The church had lost its identity as a prophetic counterculture. The political system and the church were married. The two became one.

Soon priests were approved and licensed as clergy, creating a division between men of the cloth and the "lay" man. Constantine thought the church needed to change to be "fit for a king" and his kind. The shabby houses were replaced by cathedrals. A drastic step was taken, and an institutional cathedral form was imposed upon the church. This form has dominated church life for over seventeen centuries.

Church as we know it doesn't go back far enough. I'm not interested in "improvements" that Constantine brought to the church. I want to go back to our roots. I want to go back even past the early church fathers, or even the epistles of Paul. I want to start with Jesus, and take it from there.

It was the Holy Spirit who got me thinking about the church that Jesus started. He said that Acts was starting too late. After that, I found myself racing through a radical paradigm shift. Everything was being redefined for me and I could no longer be satisfied with what "church" had become. I suspect that the future church will look more like the ancient church. We must go back to go forward.

FORK IN THE ROAD

I have this picture in my mind of the church walking down a path. After three centuries of a church without any walls, there came a fork in the road. We took a path that seemed easier, but eventually found ourselves miles away from our original destination. This path led to several derailments and to what is now known as "the dark ages." Martin Luther and the reformation of the sixteenth century caused the church to turn around and begin to make our way back. We have been heading for the original fork in the road. Only at that point can we change paths and move forward into our destiny.

There are no quick short cuts through the bushes from one trail to the other. We have to go back down the path and revisit all the errors that were made along the way. This process of rediscovery and restoration seems to be speeding up. The church is in full sprint. We're so anxious to get back on track. We began with a slow walk, but now the church, over the last one hundred years, is running. I believe that we are coming very close to where the first fork in the road was. We have to journey back to Jesus to then be able to go forward. The book of Acts was only the beginning.

KEEP IT SIMPLE

One of the things I loved about the church that Jesus planted was its simplicity. "They ate their food with gladness and simplicity of heart." (Acts 2:46). Simplicity is not the word I would have chosen to describe my own experience. The dozens of "church growth" and "church planting" books that I have on my shelf are anything but "simple." Having a church plant actually succeed, as described in these books, takes a tremendous amount of skill and resilience. Only a "super-apostle" can actually do this. I don't think the apostle Paul could have led a mega-church. He wasn't a great public speaker, was fearful, and self-conscious. (1 Corinthians 2:1-4) These are not qualities becoming to a lead pastor. I believe that in the days ahead, the harvest will be so great that every normal believer should be able to disciple the nations. It has to be simpler.

The remainder of this book is going to look at what I discovered from the church that Jesus started. We can find these just by perusing the gospels and following Jesus' example. I believe that the following seven lessons are relatively simple to understand and, with the help of the Holy Spirit, are completely attainable for any believer committed to Jesus. I've been experiencing these ancient ideas for a few years, and I can never go back. I'm outside the walls for good. Believers all over the world are following Jesus and leaving the cathedral forms behind. Many of them are from the emerging generation, which has been prepared for this journey back to the past and into the future. The church that Jesus started is the one He's going to finish with.

CHAPTER NINE

Inside OUT: They Were Amphibious

The frog is a truly fascinating creature. It begins its life as a larva and has many things in common with fish. Sometimes called pollywogs or tadpoles, larvae live in water and have gills at the sides of their heads that enable them to breathe underwater. They also have a tail that they use to swim. As they get older something magical happens.

The young larvae undergo a dramatic change in anatomy, diet, and lifestyle. During this time, the tadpole slowly changes from a fish-like, water-dwelling animal to an animal better suited for life on land. They develop lungs, lose their tails, and grow limbs. This is called "metamorphosis." Adult frogs have body structures that enable them to move about on land as well as in the water. A frog is an amphibian.

There are over 4,000 species of amphibians, the more famous being frogs and toads. Their double life is reflected in the name, which comes from the Greek words *amphi*, meaning "both," and *bios*, meaning "life." Therefore, the adjective form "amphibious" describes a natural existence in two environments. If it's amphibious it combines the two characteristics. Many things can be amphibious, anything from a vehicle to a plant. Something is amphibious because it can relate and adapt to both land and water.

Similarly, the early disciples lived naturally in two environments. They were amphibious. I believe that Jesus lived a double life. He too was amphibious. He modeled it. This was the very first lesson the Holy

Spirit showed me about the church that Jesus started.

MISSION AND COMMUNITY

Very early in Jesus' ministry He chose and called the ones He wanted to be with. After a time of prayer, He picked twelve men to walk with Him on His mission. I followed this example when we started meeting as a church in our home. I prayed about the people in my life and asked the Lord to show me who was to be a part of it. I asked four families to join us.

Mark 3:14 reveals the purpose of Jesus choosing these men. It is written there that "He appointed twelve, that they might *be with Him* and that He might *send them out* to preach, and to have power to heal sicknesses and to cast out demons." Here we have the two environments: community (being with Christ) and mission (being sent out). Jesus designed the church to be able to breathe, live, and thrive in two worlds.

One world exists behind closed doors, the private and intimate side of the church, where believers enjoy mutual exhortation and fellowship. Those on the outside cannot relate nor survive in this place. The other world is all around us as soon as we walk out the door. It's the world that we've been sent to. We can flourish here too. We are amphibious.

LOVED AS THEY WERE LOVED

Jesus chose to share His relationship with His Father with others who would be close to Him. He demonstrated an environment for community that was natural and deeply relational. In many of our church settings, this is a major area of lack. So many believers are lonely and missing meaningful friendships with one another.

"Do you love me?" This was a question I asked some of the people in our group of believers one evening. Jesus asked Peter this question that morning on the beach, after His resurrection. (John 21:15-19) I want to know that the people I'm in fellowship with actually love me and I them. I have had too many "relationships" with people that I didn't have friendship with. Why do we connect with believers? What draws us together? Is it ritual or duty? Are our relationships strategic to where we want to go in ministry or in life? Are we using each other? Do we have relationships with others because we are on the same ministry team or service project? How often do we stay connected after the ministry function is over or the group has changed? These relationships tend to be shallow. This was not so in Jesus' church. Jesus deeply loved His disciples. (John 13:1) He called them His friends, because He could fully disclose Himself to them. (John 15:15)

One day Jesus was surrounded by religious people asking Him theological questions designed to trap Him. There was one scribe that asked an honest question, "What is the greatest commandment?" Jesus gave the man the answer he was hoping to hear, "Love the Lord your God with all your heart, soul, mind and strength. And the second is to love your neighbor as yourself." (See Deuteronomy 6:1-5 and Mark 12:30-31.) This passage in the Torah was quoted twice a day by the religious, in a prayer called the "Shema." Isn't it amazing that you can know what the Scripture says, and yet not really know it? All that God wants of us is wrapped up in love. It's about relationship. Yet Jesus told the Pharisees that the love of God was not in them. (John 5:42) They knew the entire sum of the Law was found in love, yet they had no love in them.

Religiosity empties the meaning of the Scripture, and reduces love to hollow words. The religious person will not and cannot love you. My wife, Tamara, once said, "Loving Jesus without loving people is called religion." This may explain why there seems to be a crisis of love in our churches.

There is a reason why it is difficult or nearly impossible for people bound by religiosity to love. They themselves do not know or cannot receive the love that God has for them. They are struggling with God's love for themselves. The only way to really love each other is to be loved by God. Jesus raised the bar when He said, "A new commandment I give to you, that you love one another; as I have loved you, that you also love one another." (John 13:34, 35) "Love my neighbor as I love myself" is one thing. But how can I love someone like Jesus loves me? We can only give that kind of love if we ourselves have received it from Jesus. As Jesus loves us, we can love one another. This kind of love goes deeper than getting along with people you click with. In Jesus' church, a tax collector for Rome and a zealot, who hated Rome, learned to love each other. Their common ground was that they were both loved by Jesus. We love because He first loved us.

When the world encounters a believer, the word "love" should come to mind. Jesus went on to say that the world would know we are Jesus' disciples because we love. As Jesus loves on us, we can be empowered ourselves to love others with that same love.

COMMUNION WAS A MEAL

Jesus and His friends ate together often. Can you imagine in the three years they were on the road, how many meals they must have shared with each other? The most famous, of course, was their last supper. Some of the deepest revelation of the Father came to us through that meal, shared on the night Jesus was betrayed. It was there that, as Jesus broke bread and drank wine with the ones He loved, He initiated a new custom. "As often as you eat and drink together, remember me." (Luke 22:14-23; 1 Corinthians 11:23-26) The early church did not primarily gather around a pulpit, stage, or worship band. They met around a table. They shared food with each other, along with their hearts and lives. This is called "fellowship, in the breaking of bread." (Acts 2:42, 46) This simple act of friendship and family, eating around the table, is the context of church life.

Communion was a meal. The New Testament and early church history show the Lord's Supper to be a full meal. By AD 150, however, steps were already being made to separate the "social potluck dinner" from the "Holy Eucharist." Communion was soon reduced to a religiously symbolic ritual, emptied of its original power and meaning. I really believe it is imperative that we eat together regularly as believers and friends of Jesus. In Jesus' church, intimacy was nurtured by eating together as a close-knit group. However, Jesus showed His disciples that He could also naturally relate to those on the outside.

WITHOUT WATER WE DIE

Jesus openly ate with tax collectors and sinners. What was amazing about how Jesus related to people was not only the fact that He was comfortable in that environment, but that prostitutes and drunkards were comfortable around Him. He was amphibious. He was in the world, yet almost mystically, not of it. A healthy and vibrant church is one that can flourish in both environments, in our own intimate gatherings and in our mission to make disciples of all nations.

This is one of the signs that the church in the West may be in trouble. Many believers are not comfortable around (and are even frightened by) unbelieving people. There exists a deception that makes it feel unnatural for Christians to be with unbelievers. There is a false sense of comfort, when we can continue, month after month and year after year, without having any real close friends outside the church. This is not natural at all. It denies our very nature as Christians.

What is even more troublesome to me is that people who do not know Jesus often have nothing very positive to say about their experiences with the church. Whether the world is right or wrong in their perception is really not the issue. The fact is that they don't see us in a very good light. This was not the case with Jesus' church. People loved Jesus. He was the only "spiritual leader" they had ever seen who was approachable. The early church in Acts had the same type of reputation, "having favor with all the people." (Acts 2:47) In general, we haven't given people a chance to have their opinions changed by allowing them to get to know us. I understand that there are undoubtedly many believers who are exceptions to this generalization. However, there are certainly too many "non-amphibious" Christians walking around.

The truth is that if you're a believer, you're not a fish or a land animal. You should live both lives. You have both capabilities within you. Amphibians actually need to live near water for their survival. There are two reasons for this.

The first reason has to do with something called "homeostasis." All living things have this in common. They must maintain stable internal conditions to stay alive. These include heartbeat, water content, and temperature. As humans, we are designed to function at an internal temperature of 98.6 degrees F. Our bodies accomplish this through a series of biofeedback mechanisms, such as shivering when it's cold or sweating when it's warm. Most amphibians control their internal temperature through a healthy balance of time in water and time on land.

Amphibians are cold-blooded, or more correctly, ectotherms—that is, they are not able to generate their own body heat. Instead, their body temperature is determined by their surroundings. Much of an amphibian's lifestyle is dictated by the necessity of keeping its skin moist and preventing its body temperature from becoming too hot or too cold. In addition to this, their moist, hairless skin allows water to pass in and out, giving them proper internal water content. Maintaining homeostasis for an amphibious creature depends directly on moving back and forth between land and water.

As a Christian, I cannot spend long periods of time in community and fellowship without going back out into the world to advance the kingdom of God. This is not healthy for me internally. I need to get back into the water. There is probably nothing more uplifting than having the opportunity to share Jesus with someone who doesn't know Him. It's exhilarating. We were created for this. However, spending too much time in the water is going to bring my temperature down to dangerous, life-threatening levels. I must get up on land once again and let the sun warm me up. Perhaps you may be starting to get the picture.

Interestingly enough, there is another reason why amphibians must be near water. Only in water can they reproduce. Their eggs need to be placed in water, or in a damp place, to prevent the developing embryo from drying out. Staying away from water means we have no babies.

Jesus said, "Go out into the entire world." This is the only environment where we can reproduce and have more people added to the kingdom of God. We need to return to our true nature as followers of Christ. Let's get our feet wet once again and thrive out in the place where people live. The world desperately needs God's people to get back into the water.

CHAPTER TEN

OUT OF ORDER: THEY WERE CHAOTIC

"Church structure"—this is often the most perplexing question of leadership. It is in this area that we're always scratching our heads, debating, and spending long hours in secret board rooms, planning how to organize the church. How do we manage or control the church in such a way that nothing surprising happens? We don't want to be cleaning up any unnecessary messes.

Leaders are also very concerned about growth. How can we structure the church to grow? We need an infrastructure that allows the vision of the leader to trickle down the line, so that all are working together to support that vision. An appropriate structure base will allow us to emanate the values of the church in order for each individual to know how to think. Everyone will be going the same way. Assimilation is valued, and the more a person can conform to the vision and values, the easier it will be for that individual to rise up into places of leadership within the structure.

Often we see "form" as the secret to a healthy church. We want a structure that is predictable, stable, and repeatedly gives us the results we expect. Leaders fear being out of control. Therefore, our structures tend to be top heavy, focused on authority and uniformity of its members. Passive obedience makes things work much easier. A centralized command orchestrates all the activity of the church. Everything must feed back to those in authority.

We seek structures that are simple. Something that is easily reproducible. If we can draw our church format and activities on a flow chart, we are pretty excited because we can know what to expect. Week in and week out, things are fairly predictable. You can count on the programs being there, much like physical law. What goes up must come down. It is "cause and effect." If we put a certain amount of energy into it, we will always get the expected result. It's compact and neat, in a nice little package. The machine is running smoothly, and we are happy.

I do believe that structure is vital. Living things have structure. Where would we be without a skeletal system? Our bodies would not be capable of any productivity without structure. However, is the structure of life as simple as we would like it to be? When you look out into nature, you discover that all living things have this in common when it comes to structure: complexity.

Previously I wrote about keeping it simple. This simplicity is in reference to our role as individual believers in relationship to ministry and the church. For example, I do not have the skill to design and construct a computerized robot. This task would be much too complicated for me and requires abilities and knowledge I do not possess. I have helped to produce living children, however. This took less "skill" on my part and yet the product is so much more complex. The building of a machine cannot compare to the development of a baby in the womb. Yet the complex physical maturation of a child is out of our hands. It is a process that we cannot control nor manage. Likewise, the church is a living entity that can be conceived, birthed, nourished and cared for, but never created, managed, or organized by any human being. It is organic. At least this was true of the church Jesus started.

What was the structure of the church that Jesus started? It can be summed up in this concept: organized chaos. I want to explain what I mean. The Holy Spirit said to me one day, "I want you to think about these phrases: organized chaos, planned spontaneity, and structured freedom." Initially, I had no idea what this meant. As I pondered on these words, God gave me some examples that week, which really showed me what this was all about.

We held regular house church meetings scheduled for Wednesday night and Sunday night. On one particular Wednesday night meeting, I took some young people along with me that were not regularly a part of this group. The forty-five minute drive over to the location of the gathering turned into an amazing time of discipleship. It was incredible. We were opening up the Scriptures together and all of us were getting wonderful revelation from the Lord. We finally arrived at the house and did our thing. It was alright, good as meetings go. Afterward, we returned to the car and picked up where we left off. The young people were excited and before long we started to pray together. The car ride in both directions truly made the night. When I got home I asked myself, "Why did the trip to the meeting feel more like 'church' than the meeting itself?"

So a few nights later, I went to the Sunday night gathering and the same thing happened. Except this was an off night, not a good meeting at all. The entire evening seemed flat, and it felt like no one was connecting with each other or God. I taught some lesson from the Bible, but it just didn't seem to come out right. By the end of the evening I was somewhat frustrated. We want to have good meetings, right? There is this pressure that we've got to get the meeting right. We want to attain this unseen level of ecstasy, where everyone is "entering in."

So then, after it was over, I left the house to go start my car and head

135

home. One of the young men came out to meet me before leaving and said, "Paul, you seemed down that things didn't happen tonight. Are you okay? Do you need some prayer?" At that point, all the others came out onto the front boulevard. As we talked, everyone agreed that we didn't really connect very well that night. We talked for about 45 minutes out under the stars, laughing, sharing, and praying for each other. When it was getting quite late I asked my friends, "Why didn't we do this three hours ago when the meeting started?" It was as though God was saying, "Do you really think I can be restricted to your scheduled 'God' times?"

Consider the church service on Sunday morning. Whether we're a congregation of 50 or 5,000 people, do we really believe that each individual will have their personal needs ministered to? We can't even do that with ten people. It's not about the size of the group. It's about a structure that actually factors in chaos and spontaneity. I learned that the best times of discipleship, ministry and outreach are in those moments that you didn't plan on anything happening. This has been true in my own Christian walk. I have learned more and blessed more people outside of church services than I have inside the walls. There must be a structure that encourages more of these "accidental" experiences, providing limitless opportunities for ongoing ministry. These experiences caused me to ask some revolutionary questions. Could we intentionally organize the church in a way that maintains a state of chaos? Can you plan spontaneity? Is there a structure that promotes freedom?

YOU ARE A FRACTAL

The first person to tell me about fractals was Winkie Pratney. Winkie had a computer program on his laptop that was developed for the purpose of mapping out weather patterns. Weather appears to be chaotic, but what if it is actually following a predictable pattern? If someone wanted to have an outdoor wedding next year, could weather conditions such as temperature, wind, and precipitation be accurately determined for that day? Does weather actually repeat itself?

With the use of a computer, weather data from over a hundred years was entered into this program. I actually saw the shape and pattern that the data created. It was a funnel shape and had definite boundaries. However, not one single pathway was found identical to another. If you look back far enough you can see the inherent order in the weather. It has a common shape with boundaries, yet never repeating the same path twice. Weather is a "chaotic system."

Chaos math is a new science that seeks to map the nature of dynamic systems, such as weather. In this context, let me define what is meant by the word "chaos." Chaos is the final state that a system reaches in its move away from order. However, in this realm, when everything should fall apart, something strange pulls the system into a visible shape. This basin of attraction is called the "strange attractor." Though random and unpredictable, the shape never exceeds a finite border. It is order without predictability. These never repeating common shapes are called "fractals."

Every living thing, or any dynamic system, takes a fractal form. Fractal is the shape or structure of life. Clouds, trees, waves, shorelines, butterflies, dogs, and goldfish are all fractals. People are fractals. Not one human being is exactly like another, yet you can tell the difference between a person and a chipmunk. Consider the snowflake. Anyone can differentiate between a snowflake and a fern. We recognize a snowflake's identifiable shape. However, no two flakes are exactly the same. Isn't that amazing? Complete diversity and yet a common shape. This is true of all moving systems and all living things. A fern tree, for example, has branches and each branch is made up of smaller branches that look just like the larger branch. Yet not one of them is identical to another. It is completely diverse. If you examined a million ferns across the world, you find no two ferns exactly alike.

Fractals are based on simple equations that contain unending diversity. The patterns are determined by a simple rule and a series of repetitions, which feed back on itself new information. Simple repetition liberates creative potential for the complexity hidden within. Fractal art created by computer software is generated this way. Starting coordinates are entered into a mathematical equation and it sends the cursor on its way. When it stops, the new coordinates are fed back into the equation, and off it goes again. This happens thousands of times and a beautiful picture emerges. Fractal art is one larger shape made up of many smaller shapes that look like the big picture. Each one of those smaller shapes is made up of thousands of even smaller shapes that look like it. Yet not one is identical and the possibilities are limitless.

A human being develops the same way. Starting with only one cell, cell division occurs billions of times, each time using new information. Such complexity results from the relatively simple process of cell division. The simple rule that governs our physical development is locked in the genetic code found in our human DNA. We have a genetic base that makes us different from birds. There is a boundary. The two parents that we have are involved in determining what we're going to look like. Our DNA will produce only human beings, and specifically a human being that reflects the traits found in our own family lineage. Yet again, as individuals we are completely unique.

THE POWER OF THE SEED

Upon becoming a parent, I was introduced to the wonderful world of Disney. Our shelves are full of videos that seem to capture a child's imagination. In the movie *A Bug's Life*, there is a scene where an older ant teaches a lesson to one of the child ants. He picks up a small stone and asks the little ant to imagine it to be a "seed." Standing before a gigantic tree, he says, "Everything that it takes to make that mighty oak tree is contained here in this small seed!" It's the power of the seed.

Jesus used the metaphor of a seed in many of His parables. The seed determines the plant. There is nothing you can do to change that. When it comes to our relationship with the seed, we have no say as to what it will become. All we can do is plant it, water it, and maintain a healthy growing environment. In the parable of the sower, the problem was never the seed, but it was the environment that the seed was placed into. The seed of the kingdom has the genetics of Christ. What will "be" already exists there in that tiny little seed. The DNA has predetermined it.

As leaders, we cannot shape what the people we are leading will look like. The church is an organic entity, which starts with a seed. What it becomes is contained in that seed, and there's nothing we can do about that. Our responsibility is to plant the seed of Christ into the hearts of people, water that seed, and watch God make it grow. (1 Corinthians 3:

6-7) If we are "building" a church, then perhaps what we are building is not really the church at all. Who can build a tree? Who can build a body? This is outside our realm of ability.

We can touch the growth and development of organic life in two ways. We can be involved with its beginning. Life begins with a seed. Whether it is planting a garden or conceiving a child, the DNA takes it from there. Also once that process is in motion, we can provide healthy environmental conditions that sustain life and growth. As I watched my wife carry our own children in her womb, she felt the responsibility to live healthily. All living things need energy from the outside to survive. We provide our children with food and water, clothing and shelter, and a loving home to nurture their development. Plants need water and sunlight. Sometimes we provide our plants supplemental nutrients, and even try talking to them from time to time. These are the conditions of life.

I believe the process of development in the church is discipleship. Discipleship is the repetitive feedback to the equation of Christ, which involves continuously leading people to Jesus through Scripture, fellowship, and prayer. This produces the fractal shape of the church.

All living organisms grow and change. Cells divide to form new identical cells. However, they do not stay identical for long. Something we call "differentiation" occurs. This is when cells mutate into other types of cells, making more complex organisms, for example, the different types of tissues found in the body. Likewise, at first the disciple mimics his mentor and the two seem the same. When differentiation begins to happen, the disciple becomes more independent, as he or she discovers their calling and gifting. This process is natural and necessary. Relationship must change. What is important to you may not be as important to others in the body. We all have our place. Some cells are for muscle tissue and others may be for skin. However, in the early stages, who can really tell? In the body of Christ, we just don't know who will be the eye and who will be the hand. It is not for us to determine. It's all predetermined by our "spiritual DNA."

Therefore our structure in the church must be rooted in the genetics of Jesus and revolve around maintaining stable environmental conditions. A poor environment can stunt the growth of any living organism. Our role as leaders is to ensure the environment remains safe and healthy. However, the shape of the church is beyond our control. The "Jesus Seed" has already determined what it will potentially look like. This is how Jesus' church is structured. These factors are in place to form the church so that it looks like Jesus. The fractal shape of the church is the very image of Christ Himself. We are all to look like Jesus. But not one individual part is exactly like another. So relax! It's not up to you to structure the church.

LIFE IS COMPLEX

All living things are complex structures. This is even true of single cell organisms. Most inorganic things do not have this quality. Complexity and life are synonymous. Consider the most basic unit of life, the cell. In my pinkie finger alone there are over 21 million cells. The human body consists of trillions of cells. Each cell is irreducibly complex. A single cell in your body is busier than the traffic in a city. When some cells replicate, 360,000 turns of its DNA helix must be first unwound. Each of the 3.6 million nucleotides on one side of the DNA molecule must pull away from its mate. We are talking about the movements and attachment of 7.2 million nucleotides in one cell replication. The cells of your body are bursting with activity. (This may explain why I feel so tired all the time!)

Even the most complex innovation that man can create is "kid's stuff" compared to what we find in life. The computer chip is pretty amazing technology but it is still simple compared to the human brain. Anything man can invent or make is still simple, because it's not alive. We cannot create life. Life is complex.

If something has a simple structure, it is probably not alive. I could easily draw the schematic of a chair, house, or calculator. Each one is more complex, yet very simple compared to the human body. We have charts that show us representations of the body's systems. However, these diagrams hardly reflect what is really going on in the human body. They are a poor representation. Again, if it is simple and static, it's most likely not living. This is also true of church activity and structure. If you can draw out your church life on a piece of paper and it's the same every week, what you have is something that's inorganic. It's not the real church.

A LOOK AT THE CHURCH JESUS STARTED

You see, Jesus' church never looked the same from week to week. All the activity we read in the four gospels happened in only three years of ministry. They experienced a lifetime of stories in three fruitful years because they were structured in a way that allowed for chaos, spontaneity, and freedom. Relational connections and the genetics of Christ and His kingdom were the guiding factors of this church's life together. The church Jesus started was John, Peter, James, Matthew, Martha,

Mary Magdalene, and more. They were a circle of friends experiencing community and life together. Only once when Jesus took his friends onto the mountain to pray did they see Him in transfigured form. He didn't do that the week before or the week after. From one week to the next it was never the same. I don't think one day was like another. On one day the church met at Matthew's house, another day at Zaccheus' place, another on a boat, and by the sea, and on a mountain. All of this was "church."

Church is not coming to a building on Sunday. That is too simple. That is something man can create, but God's life is much more complex. Often what is called "church" can be drawn as a schematic. It doesn't matter how busy the mega-church is with its hundreds of programs, it is still not the church. The body of Christ is much more complex than that. Many of us were searching for a church that was simpler. However, if you want it simple it will not be living.

Here is a possible scenario. Your friend comes over for coffee on Monday. You have a time of fellowship at the table. You don't do it every Monday, but you did it that Monday. That was the church. You got in your car the following day to do some grocery shopping, and on the way your friend calls you on the cell phone. She tells you about the vision she had last night and the two of you pray about its meaning. You were just the church on the cell phone. Later that week, you invite a family over for dinner and remember the Lord while you fellowship together. That was the church around the table. On the weekend, you play golf with a brother in Christ and your neighbor down the street. A wonderful conversation develops about life and spirituality. This is the church on the golf course. On a coffee break at work, you spend a few minutes in prayer with another believing coworker. That was church at work.

Try not to see the church in terms of a place you go or meetings you attend, but as a network of relationships rooted in Christ. This kind of "fluid" church is organized in the sense that it is based on tangible, real meaningful relationships. It's planned because you love these people and enjoy spending time with them. However, it's completely spontaneous and seemingly chaotic. In fact, it is so chaotic that it's not manageable from a human perspective. Only the Holy Spirit could actually pull it off. I believe that the Holy Spirit is the "strange attractor," pulling this entity, the true church, into an identifiable shape. It's the image of Jesus. It's the apostolic dream being fulfilled.

Jesus said in John 3:8, "The wind blows where it wishes, and you hear the sound of it, but cannot tell where it comes from and where it goes. So is everyone who is born of the Spirit." This is a fractal statement. Jesus made a comment on His structure for the church. God's people who are born of the Spirit have this quality, which characterizes their activity and movement. You don't know where they're coming from, and you don't know where they're going. It is fresh, free, diverse, creative and spontaneous, because they're being led by the Holy Spirit. There's no telling what the Holy Spirit will do.

I desire to be led by the Spirit. I would like to go to bed each night pondering the new and exciting things that Jesus did in my life that day. My day unfolded according to His plan. I didn't know where I was going and where I was coming from. But that's the way it is for those who are born of the Spirit of God.

LEADERS WERE THE LAST TO KNOW

After the death of Stephen in Acts 7, a great persecution was unleashed by the hand of Saul of Tarsus against the church in Jerusalem, scattering God's people everywhere. I believe this was part of God's strategy. Jesus had commanded them to spread the gospel into Judea and Samaria and out to the ends of the world. They were quite cozy in Jerusalem. The church consisted solely of Jewish-Christians and I don't think anybody wanted to leave. So a little bit of trouble got them thinking differently very quickly. They scattered and took the gospel everywhere they went. The church was out on the edge, doing the work of the kingdom. Churches were popping up in many towns and cities, and the apostles were the last to know.

We are not talking about a carefully planned church planting campaign. The apostles were not in control of this. There was no way humanly possible to orchestrate what was going on. Remember, this is too complex for us to manage. The head can direct the affairs of the body. The brain is powerful enough and is interconnected to every part. The head of the church is Jesus. Only He can organize something like this. When men get in the way and act like they are the head, whatever they think it is they're in control of; it is certainly not the living, breathing body of Christ. It is most certainly some other man-made organization they mistakenly call "the church." Please don't misunderstand me. I know that there are things that we can plan and organize, but these things are only aids. Ministries and missions of the church do often need organization. However, this is not the church, but merely products or activities of the church.

So what *did* happen to the scattered Jerusalem church? Well, on one

145

occasion a deacon named Philip traveled throughout Samaria preaching Jesus to the people and moving in great signs and wonders. Perhaps one of the primary leaders of the church would have said something like, "The last time I saw that guy he was serving tables in the daily food distribution to the widows. Who would have known this was in him?" The leadership team sent Peter and John down afterward to make sure everything was alright.

The same thing happened in Acts 11 when some disciples preached the gospel over in Antioch. Once again the team sent in Barnabas to make sure the new church there had a proper foundation. Barnabas went to find Saul and the two of them stayed in Antioch for a year to teach the people. This was the pattern. It was the people of God on the edges taking the gospel out. It was much too chaotic for the apostles to control. They couldn't keep up. They were the last to know. God was doing it.

GROWTH IS ON THE EDGE

This is something else we learn from the chaos of the church in Acts, as well as from fractals. All advancement is on the edge. The growth of any fractal system or development occurs on the perimeter. The best way to see this is to consider a tree. One single shoot pierces through the outer shell of a seed and punctures the canopy of dirt above it, reaching towards the light. At that moment, early in its development, the whole tree is in the mode of growth. It is a young, tender shoot. Eventually, in its place will come a solid trunk, reaching a finite limit in its size. However, above the ground the trunk branches off into several thick limbs, each one once being a branch itself. The limb now holds many branches. This is where the growth happens, in the new shoots and branches around the periphery of the tree. The final shape that the tree takes depends on where the new branches begin to bud. They are infinite in variation.

All fractals are formed this way. The church, as a fractal, also has outer edges where the growth lies. These fractal edges represent the people in our fellowship that are out on the periphery. These individuals are not the same as everyone else. They have little in common with the rest and don't fit in. They are not good with conformity, assimilation, or towing the party line. They are often considered to be too different or even weird. Many times new believers fall into this category, since they are not accustomed to our church culture. Often new believers still maintain their contact with unbelieving friends, something that older Christians rarely still possess. These people represent the greatest growth potential of any church community.

Typically, the church structure and culture that we presently have, demands that these individuals change. We want them to assimilate. We can't handle this type of diversity. Pressure is placed on them to conform to the values of the whole. These people either change to please men, or are inevitably forced to leave the fellowship. In ignorance, we are cutting off all the shoots. We are killing the tree. All potential growth is gone.

Fortunately, although there are millions of us who haven't found our place behind the walls, we are finding each other. We are connecting in homes, coffee shops, restaurants, apartment buildings, schools, pubs and on the street. "Underground greenhouses" are going up in every city, in every land. There was no room for us and it forced us to leave the building. Many of us, however, have not perished. We have been revitalized. We have been replanted. We are growing free and wild. The Seed is defining who we are. We are growing and being sustained by the bread of fellowship, the water and the light of God's word, and the air of the Holy Spirit. It may look "out of order," but the Spirit is in control. It's God's chaos!

CHAPTER ELEVEN

Hung OUT: They Knew Their Teachers

GOT MILK?

Have you ever wondered, with all the knowledge that Christians in the West have, why we don't see more maturity? We have more books to read, audio CDs to hear, DVDs to watch, conferences to attend, and the availability of information that has privileged no generation like ours. I believe that the average Christian today probably knows more than many of the believers in the book of Acts. Perhaps when pertaining to "head-knowledge" we know more about God than even some of the first apostles. Yet we long for the level of maturity, passion, and power that the early church had. I don't think the problem lies in what we are learning, but how we are learning.

Many Christians, even after being in the church for years, feel inadequate to minister. They believe that they must learn more before beginning to serve. In our attempt to train believers in the church, our methods have communicated something else. The elevation of men or women in ministry has greatly contributed to this issue. We have a class of professional ministers that appear to be untouchable. These Christian celebrities travel from city to city showing us how to do the "ministry."

I think the church of the future will be void of "superstars." God will be doing so much; we won't have time to look at the people doing the works. The reason we have to elevate these personalities right now is because we're so bored. We've been lulled to sleep. God has taken us from the power of darkness, from the domain of Satan, and translated us into the kingdom of His dear Son. (See Colossians 1:13) Has He done this so that we could "sit and watch?" This has become the primary activity of our church experience.

We rush every Sunday morning, fighting with our spouse, yelling at the kids, so that we can get to the building on time. When we finally walk through those doors, a miraculous smile comes across our face, and we engage in the same way we do every week. We find our seat, the one we always sit in, and we watch. There we are, all in rows. We try to get our view past the head of the person in front of us. In some of our churches at least the music is a little lively, so we get to sing and clap. Otherwise, we are spectators. We sit still, pay attention, watch, and listen to the gifted person at the front who will tell us how to live. There has to be more to this.

Believers have been tricked into passivity and ineffectiveness. If we only practiced ten percent of what we know, the world would be a different place. Why do we know so much, yet little has trickled down into our experience and behavior? It's not because we are not being taught. Many of the messages coming from our pulpits are good and right. There is wonderful content in the sermons we hear every Sunday or from our TV screens at home. Perhaps, it is not the message that needs adjustment but the method of how that message is being delivered. Just maybe, the pulpits and sermons are the problem themselves, getting in the way of the content of truth being communicated. The "what" is good, but "how" it reaches us is the main topic of this chapter.

150

There is an epidemic in the church of the West. At large, we have stayed in infancy. We are in constant need of spiritual baby food. This is much like what the author of Hebrews wrote: "For though by this time you ought to be teachers, you need someone to teach you again the first principles of the oracles of God; and you have come to need milk and not solid food." (Hebrews 5:12) Here we have believers who don't seem to ever mature. By now they should be teaching others, but instead they are constantly on the bottle. "Feed me!" We hear this all the time. This is the reason why people go from church to church. It is the excuse most given when members leave a church; "I wasn't getting fed." Why is someone feeding you in the first place? Who told you that you still needed to be fed? In my own home, one of the signs that my children are getting older is that they start to feed themselves. Something is stunting the growth of God's people.

The writer goes on to define infants in Christ as being those who are "unskilled in the word of righteousness. But solid food belongs to those who are of full age, that is, those who by reason of use (or practice) have their senses exercised to discern both good and evil." (Hebrews 5:13, 14) The secret to passing from immature to mature is "use." We have to practice and use the truth we are learning. When this happens, we begin to think as God thinks, and we instinctively know what is of God and what isn't. Truth must be learned in a context of action. We become skilled in the word of righteousness by actively using it. Learning in passivity will not lead to maturity.

This is a phenomenon that was noticed in the training environments of the health profession. In medical school, if a student watched their instructor perform procedures for too long without having the opportunity to attempt it themselves, an intimidation factor would settle in.

Fear of performing the medical procedure would quickly replace any confidence in their ability to learn this skill. "I might put the needle in the wrong place. What if I kill this person?" They've watched the "professional" do it so many times, it built up fear and intimidation. So they realized that a student should only watch the procedure once, and then do it themselves. As a result, they have developed a motto when teaching medical procedures. "Watch one, do one, teach one." The best way to reinforce what you've learned is to teach it to someone else.

I believe that the body of Christ has been watching the "professional minister" for too long. We too have instilled an intimidation about ministry in the church. It is time we change our method of training. We must get back to what Jesus did. How did training and equipping happen in Jesus' church? He only had three years with His disciples and yet these men went on to shake the world. How did Jesus do it?

FOLLOW ME

In an earlier chapter we saw how Jesus chose His twelve for this purpose, "that *they might be with Him* and that He might send them." (Mark 3: 14) Jesus invited these men to be with Him. He was welcoming them to relationship. They were going to spend a lot of time together. For over three years the disciples walked with Jesus every single day. They spent over a thousand days with each other in a constant flow of life experience and conversations. In that period of time, they would have eaten over three thousand meals together. Together, they survived storms on the sea. They served bread and fish to thousands of people on two separate occasions. They stood in amazement day after day as their master healed countless numbers of physically sick and those with afflicted souls. They watched Jesus bring many back from the dead, including a little girl and their good friend Lazarus.

Imagine how many hours they spent listening to the same stories of Jesus, from one place to another. The disciples heard Jesus' teaching often enough for it to become a part of them. Not only did they have His words, but they witnessed real life experiences to match those words. The disciples walked within a living sermon. All of these experiences were so driven into the hearts and minds of these men, that years later they would recall everything Jesus had said as though He had just spoken it the day before. It was not a problem for disciples like Matthew, Peter, and John to bring their contribution to writing the gospels, written twenty to thirty years after the events. Their time with Jesus in the flesh was forever etched into their consciousness.

Not only was there an impartation of Christ's teaching on the kingdom but also of His works. Jesus implemented a style of discipleship where He modeled it and then allowed His students to do it themselves. In Matthew's gospel account, we find ten miracles recorded in chapters eight and nine. Then, at the beginning of chapter ten Jesus gave His twelve authority over sickness and demons, basically saying, "Okay, now it's your turn to do this!" This not only happened with the twelve, but a short time later, He also sent out another seventy disciples to preach the kingdom of God and to heal disease. (Luke 10:1) They were doing what they watched Jesus do. When they returned, Jesus rejoiced at the testimonies of the miracles and wonders God had done through them. It was Jesus' joy to see these men step out in ministry.

The powerful fruit and impact of Jesus' method of training on His men was most plainly seen when He was gone. Soon after the day of Pentecost, Peter and John entered the temple courts by the gate called

"Beautiful." They were going to spend time in prayer. At the gate, a lame man asked if they could spare some change. Peter looked intently at the man and said,

> "Silver and gold I do not have, but what I do have I give you: In the name of Jesus Christ of Nazareth, rise up and walk." And immediately his feet and ankle bones received strength. So he, leaping up, stood and walked and entered the temple with them- walking, leaping and praising God. (Acts 3:1-10)

Wow! This looked familiar. People had heard of stuff like this going on in Galilee. These were the works of Jesus.

The Sanhedrin soon heard about it. How could they not? It happened on their doorstep and as a result of the healing, some five thousand people came to faith in Christ. (Acts 4:4) Of course, Peter and John were brought into custody for questioning. Peter was filled with the Holy Spirit in that moment and he spoke to those religious leaders with great authority, wisdom and boldness. This was the response of the Sanhedrin:

> Now when they saw the boldness of Peter and John, and perceived that they were uneducated and untrained men, they marveled. *And they realized that they had been with Jesus.* And seeing the man who had been healed standing with them, they could say nothing against it. (Acts 4:13, 14; emphasis mine)

The Sanhedrin was shocked by what they were hearing and seeing. They couldn't believe it because these men were "uneducated" and "untrained." Peter and John were only fishermen. They had not received formal religious instruction in the recognized rabbinical schools. They had never been to seminary. How could they do the things they were doing and how did they know so much about God? Where was their confidence coming from, without having any academic qualification legitimizing their ministry? Who did they think they were? Basically, the religious voices being heard that day were saying, "You can't do this! You are not qualified."

What was the conclusion of this matter? Here we have two unqualified fishermen from Galilee who speak with authority and a lame man who is walking for the first time in his life. There was only one way to explain this, "They realized that they had been with Jesus." Over three years before this moment, Peter and John had their lives radically turned upsidedown when a man they hardly knew said, "Follow me, and I'll make you fishers of men!" Jesus said, "Be with me." I'm sure they had no idea where this journey would lead them. Now they were doing what Jesus did. I can see how threatening this was to the religious rulers. They thought they had squashed the "problem" by killing the leader. Now, instead of one man causing all the commotion, there were twelve men like Jesus. And more would soon follow.

This was a brilliant strategy. Jesus had thirty-three years on this planet. I would have set Him up with public ministry as a child. I would have wanted to get as many years as possible in for Jesus to make His impact. I would have set up a world tour for Jesus. He could speak to millions all over the world. Yet the wisdom of God seems foolish to the human perspective.

The Father kept Jesus in hiding for most of His life, only to release Him for His final three years. Jesus spent most of those last years roaming throughout the countryside of Galilee. There were not a lot of people around there in comparison to the population of the world at the time. He visited the big city a few times, but spent most of his life in obscurity. The entire world had no clue that the Son of God was currently walking the planet. Throughout Jesus' short life, He remained within a hundred miles of His hometown. He held no public position of authority. He never wrote a book. When you take into account the history of the world, Jesus' time here was only a breath. Yet there is no other man who has impacted humanity like Him. How did He do it?

He chose twelve men. They were His priority in His earthly ministry. Discipleship is about reproduction. Jesus transferred all that He had over to these men. He duplicated Himself twelve times over, creating an exponential growth potential. Although Jesus healed and ministered to the multitudes, that is not where He left His legacy. The crowds came and went, but only that which remained would prove to be Jesus' greatest contribution to the world. Jesus was focused on preparing these twelve friends. This mandate took precedence over everything. We would do well to follow Christ's example. As leaders in the church, we often think that true success in ministry is found in preaching to the masses or having widespread influence. However, Jesus taught us to disciple three or four or twelve individuals, giving them all that we have. This is our legacy. This is why there are millions of believers across the earth. It was a brilliant plan. To be "with Jesus" sure paid off, and those men went on to pierce the nations with the simple message of a crucified and risen Christ.

The invitation to "follow Jesus" is what captured the first disciples. They were willing to leave everything behind. The word translated "follow" is the Greek word *akoloutheo*. It comes from two root words that mean "union" and "the road." Together, it means to "be in the same way with" or to "accompany." "Follow Me" carries the image of walking the same road together. Jesus was giving these young men the opportunity of a lifetime. Jesus was saying, "Come and walk with Me down this road of life. Let's journey together."

The purest environment for training, equipping, teaching or discipleship is not the classroom. True discipleship does not happen in the lecture hall, or the multipurpose room, or even the sanctuary of the church building. Jesus' method of reproduction was an intimate and relational dialogue along the road of life. The place to learn the ways of God is on a walk. Imagine how many things the disciples learned just walking from town to town. Let's follow God's example and train God's people like He did. Let's get outside the building and go for a walk.

THE EMMAUS ROAD

There are just a few events in the life of Jesus that can be found in all four gospels. These are critical to the message of Christ and none of the gospel writers would have dared to leave them out. Of course, all four gospels describe the passion of Christ and His resurrection. In one form or another, each gospel references the story of Peter's confession that Jesus was the Christ. This is the place where Jesus changes Simon's name to Peter, which means "little stone." I believe that the lesson in this short narrative is critical to understanding our salvation in Jesus.

Jesus asked His disciples in Matthew 16:13-20, "Who do men say that I, the Son of Man, am?" After listening to the report of the disciples on all the diverse theories that were being circulated about Jesus' "true" identity, He probed deeper with another question: "Who do you say I am?" At this point, Simon Bar-Jonah proclaimed, "You are the Christ, the Son of the living God!" Jesus encouraged Simon by changing his name to Peter, saying, "Flesh and blood has not revealed this to you, but My Father who is in heaven…and on this Rock I will build my church."

Peter had to get it the same way we do. Christians often think that the crowds who saw Jesus in the flesh must have had an advantage. The truth is that many people did not believe, even though they saw Him with their own eyes. Even the disciples had to come to a place of faith in the same manner we do now. Jesus told Peter that "flesh and blood" didn't give him this revelation. Not even Jesus could have given him the revelation of Himself. This was the work of God the Father. Peter got it like we do today: by revelation. Our salvation experience hinges on a revelation of Christ.

Peter was not the Rock that the church is built upon. Jesus is the only foundation that can be laid. (1 Corinthians 3:11) Jesus is the Rock. The foundation of Christ comes by revelation, given to us by the Father. It is upon revelation of the person of Christ in our hearts that the Rock is laid, and the church is built upon this experience. The foundation of the church is not the teachings of Jesus, apostolic doctrine, or even the Scriptures. Jesus Himself, as the divine person, is the foundation. That foundation can be laid through teaching the Scriptures only as the person of Jesus is unveiled to the eyes of the heart. This is the Rock that our lives must be built upon.

I wonder how many people sitting in church every Sunday have a mental understanding and admiration of Jesus, but do not personally know Him. This is much too common. This lack of connection with

Jesus may be a result of our present model of training and forming people in the faith.

Jesus gave us a simple example of how to help lay the foundation of Christ into the lives of modern day disciples. It happened along a road. How fitting. Walking along the road together is a great way for Jesus to be revealed to the heart. I am speaking of the time when, after Jesus had risen from the dead, He joined two disciples in a walk down the road to Emmaus. We can pick up the story in Luke 24:13-15.

The two travelers were discussing the recent happenings in Jerusalem, when Jesus joined in on the conversation. The Scriptures tell us that "their eyes were restrained, so that they did not know Him." Jesus basically asked them what it was they were talking about that made them look so sad. Amazed that this stranger hadn't heard the news, the two companions then relayed to Him all that had happened. In their discouragement they said, "We were hoping that it was He who was going to redeem Israel." They'd heard some reports of an empty tomb from friends early that morning but weren't too convinced Jesus had risen.

It was here at this point in the journey that Jesus ministered to His doubting friends. "And beginning at Moses and all the Prophets, He expounded to them in all the Scriptures the things concerning Himself." Jesus began to teach them about Himself, out of the Old Testament. For the remainder of the trip, Jesus continued to go through the Scriptures with them. Can you imagine receiving a teaching from God Himself, which looked at Christ in every book in the Old Testament? This is exactly what happened on the road to Emmaus. They asked Jesus to stay the night, and while they were eating supper together, "their eyes were opened and they knew Him." Later on they would recall to one another, "Did not our hearts burn within us while He talked with us on the road, and while He opened the Scriptures to us?"

This is a beautiful picture of discipleship. This is a wonderful way to lay the foundation of Christ in the hearts of His disciples. This passage shows a teacher walking life's road with companions, and instructing them in the Scriptures concerning Jesus. All the while, the Father in heaven is opening up their eyes, causing their hearts to burn inside them. The Rock is being laid. Later on Jesus would appear to the other disciples and do the same thing He did on the road to Emmaus. "And He opened their understanding, that they might comprehend the Scriptures." (Luke 24:45)

Salvation and relationship with God comes by grace and through faith in Christ. This faith depends on an authentic "opening of our eyes" to the person of Christ. This revelation of Christ comes from the Father, and it lays the foundation of Jesus in us. This foundation grounds us. Our faith remains solid even in times of trouble. Specifically, the revelation of Jesus comes when our understanding is opened to the Old Testament Scriptures. The Scriptures "are able to make us wise for salvation through faith, which is in Christ Jesus." (2 Timothy 3:15) The Scriptures speak of Christ and they point us to Him. This is how Paul packaged this whole idea in Romans 16:25-26:

> "Now to Him who is able *to establish you*, according to my gospel and *the preaching of Jesus Christ*, according to *the revelation of the mystery* kept secret since the world began but now made manifest, and *by the prophetic Scriptures made known* to all nations." (emphasis mine)

The Emmaus road account speaks of the power of friendship, discipleship, and instruction in the Scriptures; the result is the revealing of the person of Jesus. This journey is about laying the Rock of foundation into the lives of the people that we lead and guide. I believe we must teach and preach Christ in all the Scriptures. This goes beyond words from lectern or notes on a page. It's walking with others on the road and watching the Father turn on the light of their understanding. It's the beauty of experiencing that moment with our friends, the hour they get another glimpse of the Son of God. The bonds of intimacy are formed, and we can all say together, "our hearts burned within us."

KNOWING FROM WHOM YOU HAVE LEARNED

Paul and Timothy had a very special relationship. On his first missionary journey Paul preached in the city of Lystra, where most likely a Jewish woman named Lois, and her daughter Eunice, were converted to Christ. Eunice was married to a Gentile man, by whom she had Timothy. Timothy was instructed in the Jewish faith, but his father refused to allow his son to be circumcised. We don't know if his father ever did come to faith in Christ. However, from the first time Paul was in Lystra, a close relationship developed between Paul and Timothy.

When Paul returned to Lystra on his second journey, Timothy had really grown in his faith and was highly commended by his leaders and local church. Paul asked Timothy, under the prompting of the Holy Spirit, to join him in his apostolic travels. Timothy became a young apostle and apprentice to Paul. Their relationship deepened as Paul emerged as a father figure to Timothy. In both his letters to Timothy, Paul calls him "a true son in the faith" and "a beloved son." (1 Timothy 1:2; 2 Timothy 1:2)

Paul's second letter to Timothy was occasioned by his concern to preserve the gospel for the next generation. Paul wrote this letter from prison. It was his second occasion under Roman guard. However, unlike the last imprisonment, this time he did not stay in a rented dwelling, but was confined to a dungeon where it was very difficult to receive visitors. Paul was worried about false teachers and the corruption of the message. Could his young coworker faithfully transmit the gospel after his death? Paul knew that his life on earth was coming to an end. He had run the race.

Here we see Jesus' model of equipping being practiced by Paul toward Timothy. Timothy carefully followed Paul's example, and it wasn't only about doctrine. Timothy picked up other things from Paul, such as a way of life, purpose, faith, and even suffering. (2 Timothy 3: 10) There was much more happening here than just the delivery of intellectual information. In another passage of Scripture Paul encouraged the Corinthian believers to "follow him as He follows Christ." (1 Corinthians 11:1) The word Paul used there means "to imitate." It is translated "mimic" in the English language. The things of Christ cannot merely be proclaimed in word only, but there must be a physical expression. We need to see what is to be learned. It must be modeled before our very eyes.

Here's my theory: I believe that we learn things through the way that the information is delivered to us. What I mean is that we not only receive the truth being communicated, but also the vehicle through which the truth is coming. The actual mode of communication is just as much a part of the message as the message itself. Have you ever heard the phrase, "The medium is the message"? How that message is delivered to us is just as important as the message. Consider the intimacy of a handwritten letter over an email. The letter, along with the style of paper and type of envelope, is as much of a part of what is being communicated as the words being written. The medium used contributes to the message.

How we learn and what we learn go hand in hand. Therefore, if we learn biblical truth sitting, watching, and doing nothing while we're learning it, we will do the same in practicing what we are learning: nothing. If truth is conveyed and received passively, it will not be acted upon. This would explain why the church in the West can learn so much and yet live so very little of it. The opposite is also true, that if teaching and learning involves active elements of participation such as dialogue, discussion, and hands-on instruction, then the truth learned will be lived out.

Timothy received what he learned from Paul out on the road together. They participated mutually in an active learning environment. It was "hands-on" training, in the intimate context of relationship. Paul and Timothy loved each other like a father and son. Paul followed the example of his Lord. Jesus modeled this style of training, and sowed it as a seed into the genetics of the church that He started.

At the end of Jesus' life He told His disciples, "No longer do I call you servants, for a servant does not know what his master is doing; but I have called you friends, for all things that I heard from My Father I have made known to you." (John 15:15) We have too many leaders treating their people as servants. Servants do not really know their masters. Masters hold all the cards close to their chest. They keep themselves closed off. We don't know our leaders. Pastors are often trained in seminary to keep distance between them and their parishioners. This is not the church that Jesus started. Jesus called His followers "friends" because He fully disclosed Himself to them. He held nothing back.

They knew Him.

I believe we need to know our teachers. Paul goes on to tell Timothy, "Continue in the things which you have learned and been assured of, *knowing from whom you have learned them.*" (2 Timothy 3:14, emphasis mine) Paul is admonishing Timothy to continue in the things that he taught him, highlighting that it was Paul who taught it. Paul is saying, "You know me, Timothy! You're my son. You know the person who taught this to you." Again, knowing who the message was coming from was as important as the message itself. We need to know the people who are teaching us. The ways of the kingdom are better "caught" than "taught."

The gospel is more than words. It is a way of life. Its power is transmitted through relational contact. It was not only important that Timothy knew these things, but that he also knew the one who taught him. Information can be passed through words spoken, but life-changing revelation comes through meaningful discipleship. It is the picture of a father training his own children. In this way, we must know our teachers.

CHAPTER TWELVE

OUTlook: They Were Ruined For This World

MY HOPE

One week before the birth of our first child, my wife Tamara had a dream. In her dream she was at the hospital, undergoing a fetal assessment. There was something wrong with the baby, but the nurse assured her with these comforting words, "Mrs. Vieira, everything is going to be alright." The next morning Tamara noticed that the baby's movement was considerably less than usual. She called her doctor and she was asked to come in immediately for a fetal assessment. It was happening just as her dream predicted.

The events that unfolded over the next twenty-four hours would be forever etched into our souls. We discovered that we were having a daughter. The joy in receiving this wonderful news was quickly over-shadowed by the dark and looming reality that something was terribly wrong with our little girl. We were sent to a specialist who looked over the ultrasound images of our child for what seemed to be an eternity. He never spoke a word and deflected any of our attempts to find out what he was seeing. In the end, after a troubling sigh, he looked at Tamara and I and said, "Your child is very sick." Those words pierced my heart like the full thrust of an arrow's tip.

Every major organ had developed with malformations. Her brain, her lungs, her heart, everything was slightly off. What happened? What could possibly cause such internal abnormalities? The specialist had seen this many times before and believed it was a genetic condition. We soon learned that our little girl had "Trisomy 13." Every human cell carries the blueprint of our development in the DNA contained in 26 pairs of chromosomes. At the moment of our conception, we receive 13 pairs of chromosomes from our father and 13 from our mother. At the 13th pair of chromosomes, our child received one chromosome from one parent and two from the other, resulting in three strands of chromosome 13. It was like throwing an extra page into the assembly instructions. The doctor informed us that while our baby stayed in the womb she was safe. She was living off her mother. However, the extent of the internal problems in her body made her incompatible with life outside the womb. She was going to die.

The doctor then gave us time alone to process this horrible news. I fell apart. Tamara held me as I wept. The pain of that moment was nothing I had ever felt before. We were devastated. All of our hopes and dreams for this precious little life were crashing before our eyes. Why was this happening to us?

A few years before this, I knew of a woman who had her baby pronounced dead in her womb. The night before she would have the fetus removed, some friends and I prayed for her baby to live again. The next day, the medical staff received a shocking surprise. The infant's heartbeat was back. She was alive! In spite of the doctor's prediction that her baby would certainly have brain damage, the little girl was born completely healthy.

There were a few individuals who told me, "If you believe, your daughter doesn't have to die" and another who said, "The devil did this to you." Both of these options only caused me to fear. If my daughter's life or death depended on my ability to work up enough faith, then I would be to blame if she died. I had to reject that idea. The pressure was unbearable. I had to believe that God was bigger than me in this. My hope was in His ability and not mine. I couldn't heal her.

The idea that Satan was responsible for this was equally disheartening. Why could the devil just waltz in and take one of my children? Were we not protected from his evil schemes? I believed that even Satan was on a leash. He could only do what God allowed him to do.

I had seen a baby raised from the dead in her mother's womb, and now my own child's life was in danger. The week between the diagnosis and the birth of our first child was the longest week of my life. There must have been hundreds of people praying for us. We were hoping that God would heal her. The day she was born was November 2, 1996. She lived one hour and died in our arms.

The next three months were dark. We were in the depths of grief. I felt like I had run hard into the sovereignty of God and it knocked me on my back. I didn't want to get up again. I lost my faith in prayer. I thought, "Why pray? God will just do what He wants anyway." Although the question of "why" was constantly haunting our every thought, we found no comforting answer. Someone suggested that God was teaching us something. However, this brought no consolation to us at all. Why did God have to kill our child to teach us? Surely He could have taught us the lesson another way.

No matter how much I tried to assign responsibility for my daughter's death elsewhere, at the end of the day it led me to God. God allowed this. I had to face the last option. God is ultimately responsible. I could be safe from the devil and even myself, but there was one person in the universe that I could not escape: God.

Believe it or not, this was the most comforting thought of all. I couldn't trust the enemy, nor could I even trust myself, but God is one I could put my trust in. I remember having a rational conversation with Tamara about whether or not we should turn away from God because of what had happened. It was such a surreal moment. Tamara looked over at me and said, "How can we run away from the only One who can heal us?" Was there really any choice? We could spend the rest of our lives as fugitives and live in complete torture. Or we could throw ourselves into His mercy and let God restore our hope. "Come, and let us return unto the Lord; for He has torn, but He will heal us; He has stricken, but He will bind us up." (Hosea 6:1) "Though He slay me, yet will I trust Him." (Job 13:15)

I saw a side of God that I had never known. He was very near to us and poured out His love and compassion over us. We experienced some of God's depths. We shared an intimacy that has changed our lives forever. This world faded into the shadows as we touched something divine, and eternity was written into my heart. There was something tangible now in heaven. She was there. The "blessed hope" that I would see her again became an anchor to my soul. My affections for this earthly life received a deadly blow. I didn't care as much about this world. I wanted the next one much more. We named our little girl Hope.

In times like this we really see what is important. I remember thinking if God were to offer my daughter back to me upon the condition that I would have to spend the rest of my days in poverty, there would be no hesitation on my part. I would take her back in an instant. All of a sudden the things of this world didn't matter anymore. I became homesick. I wanted to be with my Savior and my daughter. Suffering this pain changed my perspective drastically. I have a vested interest in eternity now. This present life only has meaning in what I can take with me to the next life. I was ruined for this world.

LIFE IS A VAPOR

The Scriptures give us eternity's perspective on the years we live on this planet. It is but a vapor and a breath. (James 4:14; Job 7:7) It's a mist that comes and goes. Isn't that sobering? When considering the reality of everlasting life, the time we spend here will only feel like a moment. This is such a small part of our existence, and yet we spend much of it fretting. Our time is so short; we must make the most of it. We must live this life in the revelation of eternity.

Have you ever had a dream that was so real and impacting, when you woke up you were sure that you couldn't possibly forget it? Inevitably the day rolls by, and by lunch time the details of the "unforgettable" dream have escaped your memory. Most dreams last less than thirty seconds. We live full lives in our sleep, but really our dreams last only a short time. I believe that God gave us the ability and experience of "dreaming" while we sleep as a picture of something greater.

We do it every single day. We go to bed and then we wake up. It's just an act in a play, a scene in a movie called life. We're going through motions and they are prophetic foreshadows of the final destiny of mankind. We go to sleep and we wake up so we have a glimpse of what it is like to leave this world behind and step into eternity, into the presence of God. I believe that when Jesus comes again, or when we pass from this world to the next, it will be like waking up from a dream. And after only a few moments with Him, we will hardly remember the events of our previous existence on earth. With each experience of the heavenly realm passing by, we will be pressed to remember the life we once knew. We will ponder within ourselves, "I think I lived that life, but I can hardly remember now."

Eighty or ninety years (if we live that long) of living and struggling and in the end, when we step into the presence of God, we will remember it as if it were a short dream. I really believe that. I believe that is what the Bible is talking about when it says "life is like a breath."

Knowing our place here on earth is temporary and our time limited to the span of a breath or a vapor, it feels silly to think of how much we worry about the things of this world. How many hours, days, and years have we spent in needless turmoil, being captured by the cares of this life? Jesus said, "Do not worry about your life, what you will eat or what you will drink; nor about your body, what you will put on it. *Is not life more than food* and the body more than clothing?" (Matthew 6:25) With such short time, it should not be wasted on lesser things.

THE COST OF JOINING JESUS' GATHERING

Being ruined for this world is one of the most shocking characteristics of the church Jesus started. Jesus Himself paid a tremendous price when He left the glory and honor of His place at the right hand of the Father. He emptied Himself and took on the appearance of a man, served the human race, and was ill-treated by the people He created. (Philippians 2:5-7; John 1:10, 11) God reduced Himself to a vulnerable fetus in the womb of a teenage girl. Jesus was born in a manger, a feeding trough for dirty and smelly animals. He lived in a world marred by sin, disease, hate, and all kinds of evil. The Holy One would go on to know hunger, pain, heartache, temptation, suffering, and ultimately death. He paid the highest price anyone has ever paid for anything. He poured out His own life to save ours.

When the time had come to begin His earthly ministry, Jesus had to leave the place and the people that He spent thirty years of His life with. He left behind His earthly father's business of carpentry to pursue His heavenly Father's business. Jesus was so focused on the kingdom of God that at times He almost seemed indifferent to His own family. There was one occasion in particular when Jesus was speaking to a multitude and someone noticed His mother and brothers standing outside waiting to speak with Him. Jesus replied by saying,

> "Who is My mother and who are My brothers?" And he stretched out His hand toward His disciples and said, "Here are My mother and My brothers! For whoever does the will of My Father in heaven is My brother and sister and mother." (Matthew 12:46-50)

Jesus was establishing something new that transcended the definitions and rules of this world. He unplugged Himself from cultural and societal values and norms to create a new culture, a new value system. He was bringing a kingdom that was not of this world and creating a people that had never existed before. He was the first of a new breed of men and women. He would lead a people who would love their enemies and give their money away to the poor. Jesus introduced a value system where the greatest person is the one who serves, the last is first, and if you want to find true life you have to lose the one you have now. Jesus lived this way. He modeled it and demanded that everyone who followed Him do the same.

Jesus was sent from the Father. He began His ministry alone, coming out of the wilderness where He fasted, prayed, and overcame the devil's temptations. His first assignment was to visit the cities and towns of Galilee. In one place the people loved Him so much they begged Him to stay with them longer. He replied by saying, "I must preach the kingdom of God to the other cities also, because for this purpose I have been sent." (Luke 4:43)

Early in His mission Jesus began to choose men who would become a part of His core group. By the Lake of Gennesaret, Jesus met four weary fishermen who had been out all night and caught nothing. After convincing them to let Him give it a try, they launched their boats out into the water and Jesus caused fish to fill the nets of both boats to the point of breaking. The impact of this miracle changed the lives of those four men forever. Jesus could even command the fish. He could provide for their every need. After this, Jesus called them to follow Him. "So when they had brought their boats to land, *they forsook all* and followed Him." (Luke 5:11, emphasis mine)

A short time later, Jesus met a tax collector named Levi. The Jews hated tax collectors because they worked for Rome. Rome was the "other," the enemy nation oppressing God's people. They were the occupation that brought much pain to Israel. Tax collectors were Jewish men who were considered traitors to their people. They had the reputation of being money-hungry, back-stabbing crooks. Jesus walked into Levi's tax office and said, "Follow me." Luke 5:28 simply describes Levi's response to Jesus' invitation when it says "So *he left all*, rose up, and followed Him." (emphasis mine)

The fact of the matter is every person who joined Jesus' church had to pay the same price. They were required to follow Christ's example and leave everything behind to join Him. This kind of cost continued even after the ascension, in the church of Jerusalem. "Now all who believed were together, and had all things in common, and sold their possessions and goods, and divided them among all, as anyone had need." (Acts 2:44-45)

Jesus ministered to anyone and everyone. If a person needed healing, or forgiveness, or to be set free from demonic influence and they came to Jesus, He would never turn them away. He accepted anyone's invitation to dinner, from tax collectors to Pharisees. He made no distinction, nor showed partiality. For hours, even days on end, Jesus poured Himself out for people. However, what would happen when one of those individuals decided not only to receive from Jesus, but to get a little closer and desire to join His team? What would Jesus say to the man or woman who wanted to be a part of His band of disciples, to join His church?

To the rich young ruler He required this: "Sell what you have and give to the poor, and you will have treasure in heaven." (Matthew 19: 16-30) If a rich man came to me wanting to join my church, I might teach him about tithing. Can you imagine what this guy could do for the ministry through financing alone? However, Jesus told the man to give it all away. Jesus didn't want a dime of it. He went on to describe to His disciples the difficulty a rich man endures to enter the kingdom. The kingdom of God demands that you give up everything to have it. It is the treasure in a field where someone sells all he has to buy that field to have the treasure. (Matthew 13:44) If you have a lot in the first place, it can be really hard to give it up. Everybody must come into follow-

173

ing Christ the same way, with nothing. The more we have to lose, the harder it is to let go.

Someone else told Jesus that he would follow Him wherever He would go. Jesus replied by saying, "Foxes have holes and birds of the air have nests, but the Son of Man has nowhere to lay His head." (Luke 9: 58-62) Jesus was asking, "Are you sure you want to do this?" "Do you know what you are getting into? You are leaving your home to become homeless." In that same passage, there are others who desired to be with Jesus, but had some pressing things needing attention. To the man who desired to bury his dead father, Jesus said, "Let the dead bury their own dead, but you go and preach the kingdom of God." Someone else asked Jesus if they could at least say "good-bye" to their family. Jesus responded, "No one, having put his hand to the plow, and looking back, is fit for the kingdom of God."

Jesus demanded so much. His words were so hard that many of the multitudes that originally followed Him forsook Him. It was hard to get into Jesus' church. The price was too high for many. This is why Jesus encouraged us to first count the cost. You don't want to start building a tower and find out halfway into it that you don't have the money to finish it. This would bring reproach to you. People would think, "He couldn't finish what he started." What king would go against an army of twenty thousand with only ten thousand men? "So likewise, whoever of you does not forsake all that he has cannot be My disciple." (Luke 14: 25-33)

When we don't count the cost of discipleship and fail to finish what we've started, Jesus compares that to "salt that has lost its flavor." Our society is full of flavorless salt, people who have "tried" Jesus, those whom the "cares of this world and the deceitfulness of riches" have drained of their flavor. (Matthew 13:22) I believe this is why the "church" often doesn't taste very good to the people of our culture. Christianity, as it is currently expressed, has suffered reproach and lost its saltiness.

I believe the cost to be a disciple of Jesus and to be in the company of His followers is the same today in our times as it was then. I know this is an idea that cuts across much of the philosophy of modern church growth movements, but please consider these words. It seems that we are doing everything we can to get people into our churches. We want to make it easy and appealing to the "seeker." Are we sacrificing quality for quantity? I believe the depth of our Christianity is proportionate to the price we've paid for it. One only has to look to the places in the world or the times in history where faith in Jesus is considered a crime by the State. Christians shine in such scenarios. This is because of the real sense that faith will cost you your life. In the West we are blind to the subtle reality that we too are under persecution. We may not lose our physical life, but the enemies of Jesus are present in our culture

I'm not saying that the church shouldn't grow or that believers are not to reach out to "seekers." Like amphibians, let us live in both environments. Let the seeker see how we live life with them in their world. Let's stop trying to bring the world to church and start taking the church out to the world. We can live in both dimensions, but the seeker cannot. They will enter the kingdom when the time is right. People out there really need to see followers of Christ actually walk in the path that Jesus walked. They must see believers who are living fully for Christ outside the walls of institutional Christianity.

Jesus' path led Him to death on a cross and He required all who followed Him to also "deny himself, and take up his cross."(Matthew 16:

24-27) Jesus taught us that whoever desires to save his life must lose it. "What will a man give in exchange for his soul?" What are you willing to give Jesus in exchange for an eternal life in God? Would you give Him your house, your car, your friendships, your father or mother, wife or husband, son or daughter? If He is asking for your entire life, could you give it to Him in exchange for His life? This is what the kingdom of God demands.

> Then Peter answered and said to Him, "See, we have left all and followed You. Therefore what shall we have?" So Jesus said to them, "Assuredly I say to you, that in the regeneration, when the Son of Man sits on the throne of His glory, you who have followed Me will also sit on twelve thrones, judging the twelve tribes of Israel. And everyone who has left houses or brothers or sisters or father or mother or wife or children or lands, for My name's sake, shall receive a hundredfold, and inherit eternal life. But many who are first will be last, and the last first." (Matthew 19:27-30)

WASTING YOUR LIFE ON JESUS

Only Jesus could inspire such radical devotion. The cost of following Him at entry point continued to produce a lifestyle of extravagant generosity and deep love in those who gave it all up. The individuals who walked closely with Jesus were ruined for this world. Their priorities shifted. Their dreams changed. This world and all that it had to offer meant nothing anymore. They had made the exchange. They hated their lives, forsook it all, to be with Him. Perhaps one of the most sacrificial acts of worship came from a young woman named Mary (of Bethany).

Mary, along with her sister Martha and brother Lazarus, were friends of Jesus. It is very likely that this small family nucleus may have lost their parents. Luke 10:38 speaks of Jesus going into Martha's house. Typically, a house would be described as belonging to the father in the home. If Martha's parents had died, as the eldest, she would have been given the charge over the home and her siblings. It would explain why Martha seemed to always be so burdened with responsibility and the cares of life.

I believe that Jesus was more than a friend to this family; He was also a father figure. He loved them and cared for them very much. One night, shortly after Lazarus was raised from the dead, they were all together with Jesus having supper. After the meal, Mary slipped away into her room to get something. No one anticipated what she did next. I can't imagine the look on Martha's face when she saw Mary emerge from her room with a container of costly perfume.

This perfume was spikenard, taken from an herb called nard. It was made in India and shipped all over the world in alabaster boxes. This stuff was extremely potent. Just a small drop would release a fragrance that would endure for many hours. It was also very expensive. The amount that Mary had was worth a year's wage. Where did Mary get a fragrance that costs today's equivalent of $50,000? I believe this was probably left to her by her parents. It was her inheritance. Not only did this perfume have great financial value, it also had tremendous senti-mental value. It was all she had left of Mom and Dad. In addition, the alabaster box was most certainly her dowry. In those days, the size of your dowry increased your options of who you could marry. This box represented her future husband and life.

It's hard to say what it was exactly that moved her to do it. Maybe it was the kindness Jesus had shown them in those years. It could have been because of the moments that Mary spent at Jesus' feet, listening to Him and receiving God's love. Perhaps it was because her brother Lazarus was right there, actually sitting at the table. It wasn't long before this that she had lost him too. They had buried him. Jesus brought him back. It could be for any or all of those reasons, but what Mary did next was completely out of this world.

Mary of Bethany came to Jesus' feet, as He sat at the table. With her alabaster box in hand, she looked at Him with intense love and devotion. She broke open the box, and did the unthinkable. She poured out the memory of her past, her most costly possession, her future husband, and her life on the feet of the Son of God. She wasted her life on Jesus. In one act of extreme love, she proclaimed with everything within her, "Jesus, you are more to me than anything. You are all I want."

Due to the potency of an entire bottle of perfume emptied onto Jesus' body, the fragrance of Mary's love stayed with Jesus all that week, in the garden of Gethsemane, and as He carried the cross down the road to the hill called Golgotha. He hung on the cross; all the while this beautiful smell remained. It was an offering of worship. He took it with Him to the grave. Jesus said of Mary's act of worship, "She has kept this for the day of My burial." (John 12:1-8) Truly this ultimate act of surrender was a prophetic scent of sacrifice and salvation. It was a beautiful smell in the nostrils of God the Father. To the disciples it was a waste, but often a waste to the world is a treasure in heaven. It will last forever.

It was this kind of devotion and sacrifice that attracted many people to the early disciples. They were considered either crazy or holy. They exhibited an "other-worldly" kind of air about them. It was fascinating and mysterious. I think of Stephen in Acts chapter seven, when he was being stoned to death for his faith. The account tells us that while he stood helpless under the wrath of evil man, he saw heaven open and Jesus standing at the right hand of God. He was consumed by what he saw in eternity. It was as though he couldn't even feel the stones breaking his body. He was ruined for this world, and with his enemies surrounding him, Stephen cried out, "Lord, do not charge them with this sin." Jesus is bringing modern day disciples back to this eternal outlook. Jesus is leading us out of the building and right out of this world.

CHAPTER THIRTEEN

DOWN AND OUT: PRAYER GAVE THEM THEIR MISSION

I used to be fairly skeptical of the prayer movement going on in the world today. I began to learn about places in the earth where people were praying 24 hours a day. For some reason I was equally intrigued by and suspicious of what I was hearing. There is always some new "flavor of the month" in the Christian culture and I thought this must be another "bandwagon." It was one that I wasn't eager to jump on. Yet I couldn't stop thinking about it. There are many movements in the world that don't include me, and I am quite alright with that. Why did I feel an impulse to join in with this movement?

Praying "night and day" was an idea that troubled me. One of the problems I see with many Christians is that we are far too busy with church activities. We have more meetings than we really need. Most people who are involved in some form of ministry in the church spend three or four evenings out a week, away from home and family. Many of them certainly do not have the time for relationships outside the four walls of the church. If the church is praying 24 hours a day, where does that leave room for loving our neighbor? How are we going to impact the world if we are locked behind closed doors praying all the time? I thought that spending that much time in prayer meetings would only keep Christians away from lost people even more than they already are. This surely will not help to bring in the harvest. Although my reasoning had some merit, there was something that I wasn't seeing correctly.

JESUS PRAYED

Jesus prayed a lot. It seems that at first Jesus kept prayer to Himself. He would often step away from His band of followers to pray, leaving them to amuse themselves for the time being. (Luke 5:16) On one occasion after Jesus had finished praying in a certain place, a disciple asked Him, "Lord, teach us to pray." (Luke 11:1) I believe they began to make a connection between the effectiveness of Jesus' ministry and His personal prayer life. They saw a correlation that was undeniably powerful. They too wanted this power. They desired to walk like Jesus did, recognizing that it had something to do with prayer.

As I read through the gospels looking at Jesus' prayer life, I noticed that something specific usually happened in the context of prayer. Prayer would inevitably lead to a major revelation of Jesus. We can see this throughout the book of Luke. In Luke 2:37-38, the widow Anna, after a lifetime of prayer and fasting, was allowed to see the Messiah. Anna's prayer life led to the experience of beholding the salvation of her people and in turn, it compelled her to testify of Him to many people.

Another significant event in Jesus' life was His baptism in the Jordan River. While He was being baptized by His cousin John, Jesus was praying. In that very moment the Holy Spirit fell on Him and out of the open heaven came a voice that said, "You are My beloved Son; in You I am well pleased." (Luke 3:21, 22) There were many people at the river that day coming to be baptized. Jesus was praying and it led to the Father Himself revealing His Son, and His love toward His Son, to all who were there by the river. Prayer came before revelation.

Jesus had special places that He preferred to pray. Mostly, He seemed to enjoy praying out in nature, in the wilderness or in the mountains.

One evening He went up onto a mountain to pray and spent the whole night there. The next morning He called His twelve disciples to Him. Together they ministered healing and deliverance to a multitude. What do you suppose Jesus was praying about the night before? I believe that God was speaking to Him concerning who His twelve were to be. He was waiting on God to show Him the men who would eventually carry the gospel to the ends of the earth. God revealed to Jesus the identities of the laborers, and the next morning Jesus called them to the task. This was birthed from a night of prayer.

In Luke 9:18 we read, "And it happened, as *He was alone praying*, that His disciples joined Him, and He asked them, saying, 'Who do the crowds say I am?'" Here Jesus was alone praying again. I believe that He was praying for His disciples to receive the revelation of who He really is. Jesus only spoke the things the Father gave Him to speak. (John 14:24) As Jesus' friends joined Him in the context of prayer, He asked them a question laid on His heart by His Father. It was this question that led to a conversation. In the conversation, Peter received a divine revelation of the person of Christ. It was then that he first truly believed that Jesus is the Messiah. I believe this was a result of Jesus' prayer time.

"Now it came to pass, about eight days after these sayings, that He took Peter, John, and James and *went up on the mountain to pray*. As He prayed, the appearance of His face was altered, and His robe became white and glistening." (Luke 9:28, 29) This time Jesus took His three closest disciples to pray with Him. In this place of prayer, Peter, James and John had a powerful experience seeing Jesus in a transfigured state. For a moment, they saw the Master in a way they had never known before. The three disciples were privy to a glimpse of Jesus in His glory and once again the voice from heaven was heard. "This is My beloved Son. Hear Him!"

Over and over again we see an intriguing relationship between prayer and the revelation of Christ. When Christ is revealed, people believe and are saved. Jesus is showing us that prayer is the key to people seeing Him for who He is. All this time my logic was faulty. I was thinking like a man and not the thoughts of God. I assumed that spending all that time in the "prayer closet" would keep believers away from unbelievers. How would both parties ever connect if one was always hiding away in prayer? What I didn't understand was that by giving ourselves to prayer, Jesus would directly orchestrate the appointment. Praying causes the connection of believers and non-believers to occur. Prayer releases the "God-moments" when the light goes on in the heart of a person, and they see Jesus for who He really is. Prayer and mission go hand in hand. Prayer gives us our mandate.

LORD OF THE HARVEST

Jesus saw the tremendous need among the multitudes that He ministered to. He spent hours and days healing the sick and casting out demons. The Lord could see that the people were weary and scattered. Jesus was moved with compassion. He had a deep concern and affection for the people. In His humanity, I believe Jesus felt overwhelmed by the crowds. He often did have to get alone to rest. As He traveled, thousands would seek out the place where He would be next and beat Him to it. They were always waiting, constantly wanting to hear Him, see Him, or even touch Him.

It was at one of these moments that Jesus looked out into the masses of faces and turned to His disciples to say, "Truly, the harvest is plentiful, but the laborers are few." I can certainly identify with those words. What troubles me most is that there are plenty of laborers accessible, but are they willing to get out into the field? You can't reap the harvest from the farmhouse. Outside our stained-glass windows are fields upon fields of souls ready for harvest. What is shocking to me is Jesus' next statement. If I were making the commentary on the fields that were "white for harvest," my next sentence would be, "So get out there! Let's bring it in!" Jesus' answer to the "plenty of harvest/not enough laborers" dilemma was shocking. He said, "Therefore pray..."

"Therefore pray the Lord of the harvest to send out laborers into His harvest." (Matthew 9:37, 38) The solution to this problem is to pray. Even though Jesus commissioned us to go and make disciples, He still reserves the right to direct the activity. Jesus is the Lord of the harvest. Jesus claims ownership of the harvest. It is His harvest. Jesus has a plan of who to save, how to save them, and who He'll use to share the good news. It's not enough to know that we are witnesses of Him; we must also allow Him to lead us in this task. He is the one who has the power to send His laborers wherever He pleases. Prayer is how we receive our orders. Prayer gets things moving. Prayer is a submission to the will of the Lord of the harvest.

I have always been fascinated by the passage in Acts 16:6-10. Paul and his missionary friends want to preach the gospel in Asia. This is where no one has gone before. I'm sure that Paul dreamed about the potential of harvesting in this huge area. Many people could be reached. Yet the Scriptures tell us, "They were forbidden by the Holy Spirit to preach the word in Asia." How strange. Jesus commanded His church to preach the gospel to the ends of the earth. Here they were on the edge of the world, seeking to obey Christ, yet the Spirit didn't go for it. So they tried again. This time they decided to go to a place called Bithynia. Once again, the Holy Spirit did not permit them. Shortly after this, Paul received a vision in the night of a man from Macedonia beckoning them to come. Paul knew instantly this was where they were supposed to go. Jesus, by His Spirit, was directing His laborers in His harvest.

I used to think that evangelism was our highest priority here on earth. Now I know that watching and praying is the most important mandate we have. It precedes all others. The great commission will not be fulfilled without submission to the Lord in prayer. The link between praying and preaching is an undeniable reality. When God's people give themselves to perpetual prayer, we will see a church that moves outside the walls. God himself will be arranging the appointments for us.

PRAYER IN THE CHURCH JESUS STARTED

The early Christians followed the example of Jesus. The church that Jesus started prayed a lot. The secret to the explosive growth of the church in Acts was the constant flow of intercession that was offered up before the Lord. The church was launched in Jerusalem out of a ten day prayer gathering. (Acts 1:14, 24) It was in their genetics. That prayer meeting swept three thousand people into the kingdom of God in one day. "And *they continued steadfastly* in the apostles' doctrine and fellowship, in the breaking of bread, *and in prayers.*" (Acts 2:42, emphasis mine)

Jerusalem was a hostile place for these believers to live. Remember, this was the city that crucified Jesus only seven weeks before the Day of Pentecost. That dark day over the Hill of the Skull, the place Jesus was murdered, was fresh in everybody's mind. Jesus was a huge threat to the

185

religious powers of the city. His followers, formerly frightened and in hiding, were now in the streets and the open courts of the temple, proclaiming the message of Christ's resurrection. The group of religious leaders, called the Sanhedrin, had to find a way to put a stop to this. So they arrested Peter and John and brought them in for questioning.

The Sanhedrin severely threatened them and commanded that they stop preaching Jesus publicly. Peter and John responded with, "For we cannot but speak the things which we have seen and heard." (Acts 4:20) After more threatening, they released them. The first thing that the two apostles did was to find the church and pray. They raised their voice to God and *"when they had prayed,* the place where they were assembled together was shaken; and they were all filled with the Holy Spirit, and *they spoke the word of God with boldness."* (Acts 4:31, emphasis mine)

At this very fragile point in the early history of the church in Jerusalem, the gospel was in danger of being stopped in its tracks. However, the church turned to prayer. It was a pivotal moment. God answered their cry by pouring out His Spirit and filling them with boldness to preach the word of God. The next day, they were out on the streets again proclaiming the good news to all.

There are so many examples of prayer leading to harvest in the book of Acts. Most of the time prayer actually happened out in the real world. You don't need a building to have a prayer meeting. The early church prayed a lot while out in the field. Acts 16 has a few examples. A young lady named Lydia, with her household, was converted and baptized after a prayer gathering out by the riverside. (Acts 16:11-15) A woman with an evil spirit was released by God's power immediately following a prayer time with Paul and his companions. (Acts 16:16-24) When Paul and Silas were in prison, their praying and singing led to the salvation of the jailer and his entire household. (Acts 16:25-34) These stories and more show how often the disciples were found praying wherever they were.

I am convinced that God is stirring up a prayer movement in major cities across the world. We must, however, be careful not to pour this wine into an old wineskin. I believe that Jesus wants to be in control of His house of prayer. This is much bigger than organizing a city-wide prayer gathering or a 24-7 prayer house. The house of prayer in a city is made up of all believers who are praying in that city. It goes beyond the borders of human organization. Nor can this be contained by a program or building. It would be impossible to track or orchestrate the activity of prayer among God's people. Jesus is the Lord of the harvest and He will be inspiring believers in groups as little as two or three, to pray together on site—at the workplace, in the marketplace, in homes, in communities and neighborhoods. He will be sending out the laborers as His people catch this vision to pray to the Lord of the harvest.

MINISTRY TO THE LORD

Although my purpose is to uncover the relationship between prayer and harvest, I do not want to communicate that outreach should be our prime motive for prayer. In everything we do, we must have intimacy with God as the goal. We don't pray to get something out of God. We spend time with Him because of love. We pray in order to be with Him. The things we ask Him for are to give Him pleasure. We desire to please Him. Let His will be done!

Acts 13:1-3 gives us a wonderful picture of this. Five men from the church in Antioch came together to pray. The Scripture shows us that they "ministered to the Lord and fasted." These men were standing

187

before God as priests. They chose to spend time with the Father, blessing Him and serving Him with prayer and fasting. This time together was God-directed. The focus was not on them, not seeking to get something out of God. They were giving to the Lord. They loved Him for who He is.

They waited on God, much like a server at a restaurant. A good waiter or waitress is watching you, anticipating what you need before you even have to ask for it. The waiter will listen carefully to your request and is responsible to give you what you've ordered. He is also eager to meet your needs and to ensure that your time is enjoyed. This is what it is like to wait on God. We are listening for the communication of His heart's desire. We are eager to please Him and to serve Him in every way possible. We desire to make His time with us enjoyable, to bless His heart.

Into this context God spoke to those five men in Antioch. The Holy Spirit said, "Now separate to Me Barnabas and Saul for the work to which I have called them." From this environment of prayer and ministry to the Lord, God released the first apostolic team to go out among the Gentiles. The gospel spread throughout the whole known world, primarily through the ministry and influence of Saul, who we now know as the apostle Paul. Half the New Testament was written to churches that were planted as a result of this commissioning. We wouldn't have half the New Testament if the Holy Spirit hadn't said, "Separate Saul for the work." All this became possible because five men had a prayer meeting one day. You just never know what God could do with willing hearts, people who are committed to prayer, fasting, and ministry to the Lord.

THE TABERNACLE OF DAVID

We have already looked at the significance of Acts 10, where Peter and Cornelius are connected to each other through prayer. Peter is praying in Joppa and Cornelius is praying in Caesarea, and God arranges a meeting. This story is another example of the Lord positioning one of His laborers into the harvest of a man, his family, and his friends. God knows who is ready to receive the gospel. He also knows who the closest available person is to deliver the message. The Father has the power to open up the eyes of an individual's understanding. The work of the gospel is truly "of Him and through Him and to Him." (Romans 11:36) As Peter did, so must we give ourselves to prayer and fasting. The Joppa experience of Peter will become the norm in the church before Jesus comes. The harvest at the end of the age depends on it.

When James heard Peter tell his testimony about what happened to him in Joppa, and then with Cornelius, he said that this was a fulfillment of Amos 9:11-12. The prophecy speaks of a day when God will rebuild the tabernacle of David so that all mankind may seek God. These verses hint that the tabernacle of David has something to do with a global harvest. I believe with all my heart the prayer movement that we are seeing in the world today is what will precede a worldwide harvest of millions of people into the kingdom of God.

On the day David placed the ark into his tabernacle, a psalm he had written was played. In this song, David's heart was revealed and its lyrics contained prophetic promises that would ultimately be fulfilled in the rebuilding of the tabernacle of David. In 1 Chronicles 16:23, 24, David tells all the earth to sing to the Lord and "proclaim the good news of His salvation from day to day. Declare His glory among the

189

nations, His wonders among all peoples." What a beautiful picture of a global worship movement, accompanied by the continual proclamation of the gospel in every nation. "And let them say among the nations, 'the LORD reigns!'" (1 Chronicles 16:31)

After the festivities of that day, David went back into his house and spent the rest of the evening with Nathan the prophet. He told Nathan how he was pleased that the ark was back, but something still wasn't right. Somehow he felt that the tent in the backyard was only temporary. It was a picture of something in the future, something more substantial. David was seeing beyond his tabernacle. He didn't feel right that he lived in such a fine palace while God was confined to a shabby tent. Nathan encouraged David to do what was in his heart.

Later that night the word of the Lord came to Nathan. The Lord wanted Nathan to pass a little message on to David. "You shall not build me a house to dwell in." (1 Chronicles 17:4) The rest of the message goes on to say that basically God didn't mind living in tents. He's always wanted to be among His people. He had always enjoyed the mobility and versatility that tents provided. However, God did inform Nathan that someone would build Him a house, but it wouldn't be David. The word of the Lord to David was, "I will set up your seed after you, who will be of your sons; and I will establish his kingdom. He shall build Me a house, and I will establish his throne forever." (1 Chronicles 17: 11, 12)

Most people automatically assume that this is talking about Solomon, who indeed did go on to build the temple that was in David's heart to build. However, this is speaking of something more than Solomon. There is a double meaning here. There is an overlap. Solomon's rule did not last forever. This passage is fully realized only in Jesus, who is also "the Son of David." God is promising that one day what is in David's heart will be built and it will last. Jesus is going to build the house that God will dwell in. It will be glorious and permanent. "And I will establish him in My house and in My kingdom forever; and his throne shall be established forever." (1 Chronicles 17:14)

A HOUSE OF PRAYER FOR ALL NATIONS

Jesus visited the temple in Jerusalem at least twice in His three years of public ministry: Once at the beginning of His ministry and then again the week before He died. In both of these instances He arrived in the temple courts to find them converted to a place of merchandise and trade. On the first occasion He was consumed by passion for what the temple represented and drove out the money changers with a whip. He was overcome by righteous anger, turning over the tables and releasing the animals for sale. It was quite a commotion. The disciples remembered Psalm 69:9 as they watched their Master tear the place apart. "Zeal for Your house has eaten Me up." (John 2:17)

Jesus is the One foretold. He has been given the task of building His Father a house. His vision for it consumes Him. The zeal in His heart for the house of the Lord caused Him to react in violent retaliation against the corruption found in the second temple of Jerusalem. This was only a representation of the true temple. Imagine the passion Jesus feels about the true spiritual temple of His church. Jesus could not help but lash out at the way God's name was being misrepresented. People were making profit from what should have been a holy thing. In His fury at the perversion of God's pure intentions for His house, Jesus quoted Isaiah 56:7, which reads, "My house shall be called a house of

191

prayer for all nations." Jesus rebuked the people for they had made it "a den of thieves." (Mark 11:15-19)

The Father's house shall be called a house of prayer. This is the house that Jesus has been commissioned to build. Jesus connects the prophecy of Isaiah 56 to this assignment. In that prophecy God has a message for His people Israel. He tells them not to count out the Gentiles or others who have been considered outcasts. This was not just about the Jews. God has always had others in His heart. "Even to them I will give in My house and within My walls a place and a name." (Isaiah 56:5) God is informing Israel that He's making room for more in His house. That would eventually be a big pill for them to swallow, but it was always in the plans as far as God was concerned. It was in this prophecy that God calls the name of His house "a house of prayer for all nations." Once again God ties together the image of prayer and the ingathering of all the nations.

God sees the church as a prayer house. Prayer is the dominant activity here. He will have a house that is eternal, where prayer and worship can be heard every moment of the day. God's house is big enough to hold people of every tribe and nation on the face of the earth. Within its walls there is room for all who will come.

PARTYING FOR JESUS

I would like to conclude this chapter by telling a story from my own life where prayer gave me a mission. I was in my last year of high school at the time. I had a few buddies come by on a Saturday night just to hang out and sleep over. While we were getting settled for the night, I was struggling with a certain decision I had to make. I decided to spend time in prayer, desperately asking the Lord for a word of wisdom. I immediately heard Him say, "Go outside and I will tell you what to do." In response, I had a slight disagreement with God about His instruction. Couldn't He just tell me while I lay on my bed? It wasn't long before I was outside in the backyard pleading with the Lord to answer my cry for wisdom.

Again I heard, "Let's go for a walk and I will tell you what to do." With a deep sigh, I proceeded to open the gate to my yard and head on down the street to walk. I was so disturbed by the circumstance that was troubling me that I didn't bother to look up at all while I was walking. A half a block down the road I noticed that it seemed awfully noisy out on the street. It was about midnight. I looked up and learned that I had walked right in front of a house where a college party was taking place. There were at least a hundred people on the property and in the home. The music was blaring and my heart started beating faster. I suddenly realized what God meant when He said, "I will tell you what to do." He wanted me to proclaim Jesus to some of these people.

So I did what any young man of faith and power would have done. I turned around and headed straight home. I was scared. Pacing back and forth on the driveway at home, I said to the Lord, "You tricked me." However, I did not want to entertain the idea that I was a "chicken," so I mustered up enough courage to go over to the party. I walked down the street, up the private sidewalk, through the front door, and into the dining room of this strange house.

Sitting around the dining room table were several college-aged students, drinking and laughing. One of them was wearing a robe and sandals, with a beer in one hand and a cigarette in the other. As I approached the table, I asked them if it was alright to crash the party.

They welcomed me and offered me a beer. I declined the offer and proceeded to tell them who I was. They were very friendly and the guy in the robe started blessing me. He said, "Bless you my child," taking a gulp of his beer, and then repeating the same words a few times over. I asked him who he was supposed to be. He replied, "I am Jesus."

At that moment one of the young ladies looked intently at me and exclaimed, "You are a Christian, aren't you?" I'm not sure how she knew but I could certainly see how God had set things up for me to share His truth with these people. I responded by saying, "Yes, I am a follower of Jesus, and God sent me here tonight to tell you about the real Jesus because this guy is an imposter." I smiled at the man in the robe and he started apologizing for his theatrics. I asked them if I could sit with them and tell them about Jesus. They all agreed and for over half an hour we talked and God began to reveal Himself to them.

I really wanted to show them how real God was. I thought, "I know, I'll ask if anyone here is sick…I will pray and God can heal them. Then they will truly know that what I shared with them is from God." It sounded like a biblical concept to me, so I proceeded to ask the question. Before I could finish my sentence, the police broke in through the front door, and told everyone to go home. We were busted. I stood in line as we, in single file, left the house. All the while, an officer stood at the door giving us the "evil eye" as we walked by. As I left, the host of the party, who also was sitting at the table with us, leaned into my ear and thanked me for coming. He whispered, "What you said really sunk in."

I returned to the friends who were waiting for me back home, wondering where I had gone. I couldn't explain it then, so I told them I would inform them in the morning. I was truly in awe of how God loved these people enough to get a nearby kingdom agent out of bed to go minister to them. I loved being able to partner with God in His dream to connect with the people that He had made for His own pleasure. Prayer had led me to them, without me even knowing it would happen. The Spirit led me to get *down* on my knees and *out* to the harvest!

CHAPTER FOURTEEN

OUTcry: They Remembered The Poor

A BETTER RATE OF RETURN

Who can deny the power of compound interest? I was a true believer in it at the ripe age of twenty-four. The pleasant gentleman who had sold me life insurance carefully and methodically explained over several appointments that if I committed to putting away only a minimal monthly amount into a retirement investment fund, by the time I was sixty-five I would have hundreds of thousands of dollars to my name. I would ensure a prosperous future in my latter years. If I didn't plan now, how would I survive economically when I was old?

My decision was made. I was going to meet with my financial planner that very week and secure my retirement income. I was assured by an expert that the risk would be negligible when considering such a long period of time. The money that I invested would be there for me when I retired, and I could expect an annual average return rate of ten percent. I felt very positive that I was doing the right thing. It was logical and responsible. I believed that I was being a good steward of the resources that God had given me. That was before everything was turned inside out. It all changed for me when I read a simple verse of Scripture the day before I would sign on the dotted line. I began to see that God had different ideas on what I should do with that monthly allotment of funds.

I don't know exactly how I found this verse, but I do remember it being the first time I had noticed it. Upon reading it, the words leapt off the page and pierced my soul with a challenging invitation. Proverbs 19: 17 says, "He who has pity on the poor lends to the Lord, and He will pay back what he has given." I heard the voice of God speak strongly in my mind and heart at that very moment saying, "If you took the money you are planning to put away for your retirement and instead gave it to the poor, do you think I could give you a better rate of return?"

The Holy Spirit was leading me to face what I actually believed. Could I trust God to take care of my future if I took care of the poor? I would be wasting that money from an economic point of view. The poor would never be able to pay it back. I'd be throwing it all away. It was a turning point for me in my walk of faith. Was God more real than the stock market and God's word more than the proven principles of compound interest? I could watch my investment grow over time. I could take care of myself in the years when I will be most vulnerable. God was asking me in that moment to voluntarily withdraw my own attempt at securing my future. Father strongly advised me to consider my actions and to invest into eternity by remembering the poor. The Lord would be my retirement safety net.

RED LETTER ECONOMICS

In many Bibles the words of Jesus are offset in red. Have you ever taken a period of time just to read "red letter" verses, the direct speaking of Jesus? Over the past twenty years, I have taken regular "seasons" of time to read over the four gospel writings. I would saturate myself in the parables and discourses that have come to us from the lips of our Master. Nothing has inspired me and pierced my heart like the words in red. You cannot read the words of Christ without truly being impacted at a heart level. If what Jesus has to say here doesn't literally tear your world apart, then you probably don't really understand it. His thoughts and actions were (and are) absolutely revolutionary. He showed us that a man could overcome evil with good and topple hatred with love. Jesus' message was the kingdom of God.

The kingdom of God encapsulates what Christ has to tell us. This is the realm of God's loving reign. The kingdom is the expression of God's will and organic design. Jesus' parables and teachings about the kingdom reveal God's fathering heart and how He thinks about living. Jesus' ideas are so opposed to what we have been trained to think by the world-system that Anabaptist Donald Kraybill calls it the upside-down kingdom.

Kingdom priorities, values, and practices are completely against the current of self-interested human cultures. In God's estimation, the last are first, the poor are blessed, the servant is the greatest, and to find your life you must lose it. I find most of Jesus' conclusions utterly shocking. Jesus' discourse found in Matthew 5-7 (typically called The Sermon on the Mount) reads like a magnum opus for living in the habitat (or reign) of God. Jesus speaks here about love, forgiveness, praying and fasting, and shows us how to respond to our enemies. It seems that most of all, Jesus has something to say here about money.

Jesus goes after issues of the heart. He spends much time addressing the topic of wealth and our attitudes toward it. Jesus appeals to our need to invest by directing us to "lay up for yourselves treasure in heaven" in Matthew 6:19-21. The logic of the kingdom says, "Why put your heart into something as fleeting as the structures created by the lesser principalities and powers?" Decay, thieves, natural disasters, economic crashes, and many other forces seek to destroy what we store up through conventional wealth-building means. If God's habitat is closer to us than our very breath, then it doesn't make sense to invest into something so unstable and temporary.

Jesus emphasized this dimension many times throughout His earthly ministry. Once, Jesus spoke of a rich fool. This man was so prosperous that he couldn't contain the blessing. His barns were not big enough to hold the plentiful yield of his crops, so he decided to pull them down and build bigger ones. It makes sense, doesn't it? He was expanding his business. He was taking care of himself and his family for a long time to come. The rich man said to himself,

'Soul, you have many goods laid up for many years; take your ease; eat, drink, and be merry.' But God said to him, 'Fool! This night your soul will be required of you; then whose will those things be which you have provided?' Jesus warned, 'So is he who lays up treasure for himself, and is not rich toward God.' (Luke 12:13-21)

Being rich toward God and laying up treasure in heaven comes into existence through sharing our resources with those who are in need. Blessing the poor is the fundamental expression of the kingdom and the heart of the gospel itself. Jesus began His discourse on the mount with "Blessed are you who are poor, for yours is the kingdom of God." (See Luke 6:20.) The gospel of the kingdom is about a great exchange of wealth. "For you know the grace of our Lord Jesus Christ, that though

He was rich, yet for your sakes He became poor, that you through His poverty might become rich." (See 2 Corinthians 8:9.) When we bless the poor we are acting like Jesus. We are doing in a small way what He did for humanity.

Remembering the poor is in itself a proclamation of the good news found in Jesus. Giving to the poor is preaching the gospel with action. It demonstrates what Jesus did for us through the cross. Serving the poor also involves a death for us. We are choosing to be in need ourselves so that we can give what we have to someone less fortunate. Jesus emptied Himself, leaving the glory and wealth of heaven in order to bless the poor by serving them.

Scripture tells us that Jesus endured execution for the joy set before Him. (See Hebrews 12:2.) Jesus saw something beyond the price He was paying; Jesus was living out His own teaching of the kingdom. His very life was being spent for something that would last. Jesus was laying up a treasure for Himself in eternity. This treasure is you and I. In Ephesians 1:18 Paul prays that churches would know "what are the riches of the glory of His inheritance in the saints." Jesus has riches laid up in an inheritance for Himself. This inheritance is glorious and God wants us to pierce the mystery: The inheritance of Christ is in the saints. We are Christ's eternal reward. We are His riches. "[Jesus Christ,] who gave Himself for us, that He might redeem us from every lawless deed and purify *for Himself His own special people.*" (Titus 2:14a, emphasis mine)

Jesus told His apprentices, "If anyone desires to come after Me, let him deny himself, and take up his cross, and follow Me." (See Matthew 16:24.) The invitation to follow Jesus means doing what He did. Being a disciple of Christ will inevitably lead us down the same road that Jesus walked. "Jesus people" do what Jesus does. This means we choose to take resources that we would spend on ourselves and give them to the poor. This is exactly what Jesus told the rich man who desperately wanted to follow Him. "Go, sell what you have and give to the poor, and you will have treasure in heaven; and come, follow Me." (See Matthew 19:21.) In fact, Jesus went on to tell His disciples of the conflict between the kingdom of God and the deceitful pull of wealth on the heart of a man seeking it. "It is hard for a rich man to enter the kingdom of heaven." (Matthew 19:23) In the story commonly called the "Parable of the Sower," Jesus identified a key enemy of the message of the kingdom. "Now he who received seed among the thorns is he who hears the word, and the cares of this world and the deceitfulness of riches choke the word, and he becomes unfruitful." (Matthew 13:22)

DON'T WORRY

Perhaps seeking riches is not why most people hold back from the poor. If you are like me, it was *fear* that held me captive. I once heard Jackie Pullinger say, "The spirit of poverty is the fear of not having enough." People fear that if they give they may not have a sufficient amount to survive themselves.

> Do not fear, little flock, for it is your Father's good pleasure to give you the kingdom. Sell what you have and give alms; provide yourselves money bags which do not grow old, a treasure in the heavens that does not fail, where neither thief approaches nor moth destroys. For where your treasure is, there your heart will be also. (Luke 12:32-34)

I should finish my story because it speaks to this matter of fear. I wrestled with God's invitation to invest in eternal realms (instead of retirement) for a long time. It took me two months to overcome my anxiety of not intentionally providing for myself a nest egg for the future. How could I believe that wasting money on the poor would ensure financial security for me in my later life? However, I finally yielded to Father's heart and shortly after this very difficult soul-searching experience, my wife and I both agreed to remember the poor. It was really the first time for us. Instead of setting that money aside into a retirement savings plan, we took that same monthly dollar amount and committed it to sponsoring two children through World Vision's child sponsorship program. This truly was a critical moment in our journey together. My fear of "being without" in the future melted away through a wonderful assurance in the faithfulness of God.

Years later, we did come to a place where we were free to put money away for the future. However, at the time, God was challenging us to put first things first. God turned my heart the day He showed me His love for the poor and my responsibility to help those in need.

Fear is what keeps many of us from being generous. We feel that if we give our money away, we will not have enough to meet our own needs. This anxiety keeps us tight-fisted when we see others who are lacking material provision. My experience struck a blow to this fear. In fact, our early years of marriage were characterized by constant financial difficulty. My wife and I continuously fought about money, more specifically the lack of it. The cares of this life laid heavy burdens upon us, compounded by the paralyzing fear of not having enough to pay the bills. We struggled a lot until we started giving regularly to the poor. Our financial records clearly indicate that the very month we began sponsoring needy children, there was a considerable increase in our income.

The Scripture above was a great encouragement to me. Jesus actually said that by giving to the poor we secure treasure in heaven, as well as providing a money bag that doesn't ever run dry. Giving generously to the poor is a smart financial move. God will take care of your needs if you take care of the poor.

Back in His great sermon, Christ also instructed us not to worry about what we will eat, drink, or wear. Jesus reminded us of how the Father cares for us and repeats "Do not worry" four times in this brief passage. God will take care of our life necessities. The bills will be paid. Don't try to figure out how it is all going to come together. Don't be afraid. God is real and His care for you is real. We are given a charge: "Seek first the kingdom of God and His righteousness, and all these things shall be added to you." (Matthew 6:33) As our hearts and actions are rooted in God's habitat our Father in heaven will take care of our needs.

There are many Scriptures that speak to our fear of poverty. Many use these verses to preach a prosperity message that flows in the spirit of greed and the pursuit of wealth. These verses are not meant to tempt you to lust after riches. They are loving encouragements from God to overcome your fear of poverty. The Scriptures are telling us not to be afraid to give generously. There is no need for self-preservation and conservatism when it comes to being a blessing to others who are less fortunate. When God sees His children be generous in the true spirit of the gospel, it touches God's own generous heart. God blesses those who bless others.

Honor the LORD with your possessions, and with the first fruits
of all your increase; so your barns will be filled with plenty, and
your vats will overflow with new wine. There is one who scatters,
yet increases more; and there is one who withholds more than is
right, but it leads to poverty. The generous soul will be made rich,
and he who waters will also be watered himself. (Proverbs 3:9,
10; 11:24, 25)

I'M NOT RICH!

James was another member of the church that Jesus started. James
had much to say about the poor. His letter, as a part of the Scriptures,
helps us to see a balance in the area of faith. I can relate to James because
he was a man concerned about the expression of Christianity in his generation. He addressed the issue of people who confess faith in Christ
yet do not reflect it in their lifestyle. He wrote that even demons believe
in God, but that doesn't mean they are redeemed. James' message to us
is that faith—if it is real—will show itself in our actions. True faith is
not cognitive subscription to tenets of belief, but it is a heart level trust
in the person of Christ that results in a change inside and out. We are
not saved by works, but if we truly believe and are saved good works will
flow from us. Living works are the proof that our faith is authentic.

What does it profit, my brethren, if someone says he has faith but
does not have works? Can faith save him? If a brother or sister
is naked and destitute of daily food, and one of you says to them,
'depart in peace, be warmed and filled,' but you do not give them

the things which are needed for the body, what does it profit? Thus also faith by itself, if it does not have works, is dead. (James 2:14-17)

I believe that our attitudes toward the poor may be the clearest indication of the condition of our hearts before God. To be a true apprentice of Jesus means remembering the poor. James put it this way: "Pure and undefiled religion before our God and Father is this: to visit orphans and widows in their trouble, and to keep oneself unspotted from the world." (James 1:27) I suppose this is the one verse in the Bible that talks about religion in a positive way. If religion means caring for those who are in need and living a lifestyle that stands out because of our deep faith in Christ, then we have something real here. Everything else belongs in the trash.

God revealed something to me out of James 5. The chapter begins: "Come now you rich, weep and howl for your miseries that are coming upon you." It is clear that this portion of James is addressed to the rich. Typically, I would read the warnings of this verse (or others like it) and immediately apply it to someone else. I had never thought of myself as belonging to the "rich." Not long ago, I watched a television program that praised the spending habits of a very successful box office celebrity. He received 30 million dollars for his last movie. He owns and drives eleven Hummers. He spends over $100,000 a year just to pay someone to keep his vehicles clean. This movie star has a few multi-million dollar homes in various desirable locations, hardly living in any of them. Also, he collects wrist watches that cost half a million dollars a piece. He is rich! This is who James is warning here. I'm just an average middle class guy, trying to pay the bills. When I think of the rich, someone like

Bill Gates comes to mind. He has more wealth than some countries. So I can pass over these verses and read something else, right? However, that night the truth finally caught me in my deception.

This was the first time I read James 5 and thought, "Oh no, this is me! This passage is speaking to me." Comparing my economic status to Bill Gates may get me off the hook in my mind's eye; however, what happens when I include the rest of the planet? Just where do I fit when considering the wealth of the world? Everything changes, if you read James 5 with a global perspective.

There is a website called www.globalrichlist.com, where you can enter your annual salary to see how you compare to the rest of the world. When I typed in the amount of my previous year's income, I couldn't believe what I discovered. My place in the world's economy was within the top 6.97% of the richest people on earth. There are 5,581,433,823 people poorer than me. The poorest 85% of the world makes an average of $2,182 per year, according to the World Bank. Our greed in the West keeps us looking at those who are wealthier, making us feel poor and wanting. The truth is that we are very rich.

"Today, across the world, 1.3 billion people live on less than one dollar a day; 3 billion live on under two dollars a day; 1.3 billion have no access to clean water; 3 billion have no access to sanitation; 2 billion have no access to electricity."[1] In contrast, the world's three richest people have wealth greater than the combined Gross Domestic Product (the value of all goods and services) of the world's 48 poorest nations (i.e. a quarter of the world's countries).[2] The world's 497 billionaires in 2001 registered a combined wealth of $1.54 trillion, which is greater than the combined incomes of the poorest half of humanity.[3] If the entire population of the world was represented by a tribe of one hundred people—an idea developed by Philip M. Harter, an M.D. at the Stanford University School of Medicine—six of those members would be American. Yet those six would control 59% of the wealth of the whole village.

Here, in the wealthiest nations of the world we don't really understand the nature of true poverty. Poverty is experiencing a constant state of hunger. Poverty is the lack of shelter. Poverty is being ill without any possibility of seeing a doctor. Poverty is not being able to go to school and not knowing how to read. Poverty is having no job in sight, fear for the future, and living one day at a time. Poverty is losing a child to illness brought about by unclean water. Poverty is powerlessness. In poverty, there is no freedom.

According to UNICEF, 30,000 children die each day due to poverty. And they, "...die quietly in some of the poorest villages on earth, far removed from the scrutiny and the conscience of the world. Being meek and weak in life makes these dying multitudes even more invisible in death." That is about 210,000 children each week or just under 11 million children under five years of age, each year.[4]

James is speaking to you and me. He addresses those of us who are privileged to have been born in wealthy nations. His message to us is a call to repentance. "Come now you rich; weep and howl for your miseries that are coming upon you." This is a warning that judgment is coming against the rich.

THE SIN OF SODOM

It was while I was reading this same passage in James that God led me to the revelation of the sin of Sodom and Gomorrah. You must be wondering what Sodom has to do with James. Let's follow the same trail that the Holy Spirit led me on.

There was one thought in the fourth verse of James 5 that launched me on a journey back to Sodom. Remember, God is issuing a warning of judgment and a call for repentance to the rich. He then uncovers the unjust manner in which they treat those working for them.

> Indeed the wages of the laborers who mowed your fields, which you kept back by fraud, cry out; and the cries of the reapers have reached the ears of the Lord of Hosts.

The poor man, who is working for the rich and being mistreated and defrauded, is crying out to God. God responds to the cry for justice, and this is what sets His judgment in motion. The poor and victims of injustice seem to have direct access to the ear of God. It's in God's nature to act on their behalf. Furthermore, James uses a specific name designation of God when the poor cry out to Him for restitution. "The Lord of Hosts" is a military title for God. You don't want to be an enemy of this Man of war.

James is not presenting a new idea. In the Law, God clearly laid down protocol for those with wealth on how to deal with anyone poor they've hired.

> You shall not oppress a hired servant who is poor and needy, whether one of your brethren or one of the aliens who is in your land within your gates. Each day you shall give him his wages, and not let the sun go down on it, for he is poor and has set his heart on it; lest he cry out against you to the Lord, and it be sin to you.

OUTcry: They Remembered The Poor

(Deuteronomy. 24:14-15)

God's heart here is for the rich to take care of the poor; to be fair, honest, and prompt on their payment. This command in the Torah was given to ensure good treatment of the poor, whether an Israelite or a foreigner. The sun cannot go down without that day's wages being paid out. The poor are counting on that provision for their daily bread. Can you hear the warning in this command? God basically tells us that if we don't act appropriately in this matter, the poor will cry out to Him about it, and God will consider it sin on our part. Upon hearing the cry of the poor against the rich, God holds the rich responsible. The cry of the poor is loud and clear in the ears of God. Indifference may be our greatest fault. We must be careful not to neglect the poor through self-indulgence and unconcern for the welfare of others. God is listening to any legitimate complaint they may make against us.

I believe that what is happening in James 5 is a direct application of Deuteronomy 24:15. There is a cry that has gone out against the rich, coming from the poor, and reaching the attention of God. As a direct response to this cry, God is warning the rich of impending judgment. "Weep and wail. You have laid up treasures in the last times. You live on the earth in luxury and pleasure." This is where we get closer to Sodom. Follow me back to Genesis.

In Genesis 13:10-13, we can find Abraham actually in the land that God promised to him and his descendents. Abraham was instructed to leave his family behind and move on to settle in this foreign country. However, he took his nephew Lot with him which became a problem. Abraham's family and Lot's family were both very large. They had many people and possessions to travel with; it ultimately caused tension between them. So, Abraham told his nephew, "Go and pick a place where you want to live and I'll live somewhere else, but we must separate." Verse ten shows us what happened next, "Lot lifted his eyes and saw all the plain of Jordan, that it was well watered everywhere (before the Lord destroyed Sodom and Gomorrah)..." Maybe you didn't notice this before, but Sodom and Gomorrah were actually once very prosperous and fruitful places. Lot does proceed to make his home here in the plain of Jordan because it was a desirable location to live. Lot would have a good life in Sodom. Here his wealth would flourish.

This is not what many of us think of when "Sodom" is mentioned. I would never picture it being a city of beauty and prosperity. Sodom and Gomorrah are forever a symbol of God's disdain for wickedness and evil in the hearts of men. Fire and brimstone is what this place is remembered for. However, in the narrative we must not forget God's propensity for mercy in the face of provocation from sinful behavior. God would have spared the entire region for only ten righteous people.

God revealed to Abraham, "Because the outcry against Sodom and Gomorrah is great, and because their sin is very grave, I will go down now and see whether they have done altogether according to the outcry against it that has come to Me; and if not, I will know." (Genesis 18: 20, 21) Somebody had cried out to God here. There were people with a complaint about Sodom. The Lord had not only heard this "outcry," but informed Abraham that He would go down to check this out. If the accusation was indeed legitimate, God would destroy the cities. When the two angels came to visit Lot in Genesis 19:13, they said, "For we will destroy this place, because the outcry against them has grown great before the face of the LORD, and the LORD has sent us to destroy it."

I think you can probably guess where I'm going with this. James said that when the poor cry out against the rich, the rich must be warned. The judge is standing at the door. We discovered this same principle in Deuteronomy, when verifiable accusations are aimed toward the wealthy. God sees the rich man's neglect of his poor employee as sin. Now here we have Sodom, a prosperous place, and we know that God destroyed the city because of some kind of outcry against it. Can I support the claim that perhaps it was because the people of Sodom, though having the means, did not remember the poor, resulting in the "outcry" and the city's fatal end? Is the outcry against Sodom coming from the poor in surrounding nations? Is the neglect and oppression of the poor the sin of Sodom? The story itself, as recorded in Genesis, does not give us certainty that this is the case. In a court of law we would call this "circumstantial evidence." What we need is a direct statement from God Himself. In fact, such a testimony does indeed exist!

Hundreds of years after the event, God made a statement as to what the sin of Sodom truly was. Found in Ezekiel 16:48-50, God compared the nation of Israel to Sodom. The whole chapter describes Israel as being an unfaithful and adulterous wife, who would not escape imminent judgment. This was the condition of God's people before the Lord caused them all to be carried away captive to exile in Babylon.

'As I live,' says the Lord, 'neither your sister Sodom nor her daughters have done as you and your daughters have done. Look, this was the iniquity of your sister Sodom: She and her daughter had pride, fullness of food, and abundance of idleness; neither did she strengthen the hand of the poor and needy. And they were haughty and committed abomination before Me; therefore I took them away as I saw fit.'

We've been told that the sin of Sodom was homosexuality. Sexual immorality was certainly part of the wickedness that the people of this ancient city engaged in. However, at the heart of the matter this was not what God saw as their primary error. I believe that the sexual sins associated with Sodom were only some of the fruit on this mature tree of wickedness. The root of this tree was something much more subtle, yet in the eyes of God the true downfall of this culture. They were arrogant, thinking of themselves much more highly than they ought. The people of Sodom were overfed, relished in their plenty, enjoyed prosperous ease, lived for pleasure and comfort, and sought continual entertainment to numb their minds from their perpetual state of boredom. They had everything they could ever want, and yet remained completely unconcerned and indifferent to those in need. They did not strengthen the hand of the poor and the needy. The poor cried out against them. This is what I believe: the poor cried out against Sodom and the Lord heard the cry and acted upon it.

When I read James 5, I felt warned by the Lord: "You have to set yourself apart from this, because judgment is coming to the rich." After feeling myself enter into a mild state of panic, I calmed down enough to ask what I can do to prepare for this. What act of humility could be done to preserve my family and me from this judgment that is coming? Please understand that I do not normally think this way. I've never liked the idea of judgment. I don't get a kick out of talking about it. I am not into scaring people. However I cannot ignore what God has shown me. This is hitting me where I live. I am not pointing any fingers. They are all pointing at me. The truth is there is a cry coming before the Lord in the earth from billions of the poorest people.

It seems the church may be completely oblivious to the reality of coming judgment. Not only are we unprepared for this, most of us have no grid to understand that God is capable of bringing judgment. Yet the revelation of God as a righteous judge has solid biblical support. We tend to ignore the passages of Scripture that we don't like or understand. Furthermore, we dismiss those who trumpet the warning of coming judgment and call for repentance. We think they are negative, critical and legalistic people, who spend too much time looking at what is wrong and not loving the body of Christ. This is still how I'm bent to view "doomsday preachers." Yet here I am. I do not feel comfortable with this role. I'm not one that easily handles rejection or being misunderstood. My hope is for you reading this to hear the heart of what God is saying. Father loves us all, and He also loves the poor.

Jesus talks about Sodom a couple of times as recorded in the gospel narratives. In Luke 17:28-33, Jesus links what happened at Sodom to the end times. I believe this story of Sodom and Gomorrah is a small picture of Jesus' bodily return:

> Likewise as it was also in the days of Lot: They ate, they drank, they bought, they sold, they planted, they built; but on the day that Lot went out of Sodom it rained fire and brimstone from heaven and destroyed them all. Even so will it be in the day when the Son of Man is revealed.

They were going on with business as usual, doing the things that wealthy societies do, utterly oblivious to the shocking reality of the coming of Christ. Then suddenly it all comes to an end. Jesus revealed to us that the days before His return are going to be similar. Sodom is a picture of earth at the end. Prosperous people and nations who are bound by their own self-interests and are not free to share the resources they have are going to be in the line of fire.

> In that day, he who is on the housetop, and his goods are in the house, let him not come down to take them away. And likewise the one who is in the field, let him not turn back. Remember Lot's wife. Whoever seeks to save his life will lose it, and whoever loses his life will preserve it.

As a way of preparation, Jesus is instructing us not to be attached to our possessions. We cannot afford to put our life into the power structures of this world. We must not find our security and identity in the Sodom of our time. Lot's wife was on her way out, escaping the judgment, but looked back because of her unhealthy attachment to Sodom's way of life. Her heart was still in Sodom. There was something of Sodom still in her. She turned back and became a pillar of salt.

Jesus is telling us what we ought to do to be protected from this deception. We must purpose in our heart to not be attached to our things. We have to disengage from the spirit of consumer culture, the spirit of Sodom. We need to break away from it in our hearts. There can be no turning back when Christ appears. He is returning to those whose hearts are fully His, caring about the same things He cares about. "Whoever seeks to save his life will lose it. Whoever loses his life will preserve it." The poor can help us do this. The poor give us an opportunity to give our blessings away, further distancing ourselves from greed and hoarding.

"I COULD HAVE SAVED MORE"

To help me feel the severity of what I must do with my wealth I sometimes put in my *Schindler's List* DVD and watch the final scene. Steven Spielberg did a masterful job at bringing this true story to life. Schindler was a German who initially saw the war (World War II) as a means to gaining wealth. As his business grew, the Nazi plot to eradicate Jews unfolded, and Schindler's ambition to make money slowly shifted toward a campaign to save lives. He used his wealth to buy Jews for "free" labor in his factory. Undetected by the Nazi Germans, who thought it a good use for Jews, Schindler was able to save over eleven hundred people from certain death in concentration camps. By the end he had spent all he gained, and when the war was over suddenly Schindler was considered a war criminal.

In the last scene, the hundreds of Jews that Schindler saved surrounded him in the middle of the night to say goodbye. They thanked him with a special gift of a ring and a letter signed by each one of them, explaining his innocence, in the event of his capture. Schindler, overwhelmed with intense emotion, looked at his Jewish friend, and said, "I could have saved more. I wasted so much." He looked at his car, "ten more lives." He pulled a gold pin from his jacket, "two more lives…at least one…one more life." This broken man fell to the ground and wept. He realized that every dollar spent on excess equated to lives being lost.

Jesus said, "Sell what you have and give it to the poor…" (Luke 12:33) He is showing us how to withdraw our money from the world system and invest into the kingdom of heaven. Here is a practical application of what is needed to preserve those of us who live in "Sodom."

We can shield our households from the coming disaster by liquidating our assets to help the poor. Our possessions represent funds that can be translated into saving lives. As Schindler realized, lives can be saved if we only choose not to waste our resources. As I look around my home, I see how much I have locked up in material things that could be used to feed someone who is starving or care for a child that is all alone in this world. God help us as Christians to respond to Jesus' words and sell it all. The poor are waiting for our reply. Will we remember them?

NOTES:
1. James Wolfenson, *The Other Crisis*, World Bank, October 1998, quoted from *The Reality of Aid 2000*, (Earthscan Publications, 2000), p.10
2. Ignacio Ramonet, "The Politics of Hunger," *Le Monde Diplomatique*, November 1998
3. John Cavanagh and Sarah Anderson , *World's Billionaires Take a Hit, But Still Soar, The Institute for Policy Studies*, March 6, 2002
4. See the following:
• Progress of Nations 2000, *UNICEF*, 2000;
• Robert E. Black, Saul S. Morris, Jennifer Bryce, *Where and why are 10 million children dying every year?*, *The Lancet*, Volume 361, Number 9376, 28 June 2003. (Note, while the article title says 10 million, their paper says 10.8 million.)
• *State of the World's Children*, 2005, UNICEF (this cites the number as 10.6 million in 2003)

CHAPTER FIFTEEN

OUTSPOKEN: THEY HAD A VOICE TO THE CULTURE

A few years back I had some friends over at the house to hear my life story and listen to some of the music I had written. They were all in their early twenties, and I learned quickly what they loved to do. Every Monday night was "Techno Night" at one of the local night clubs. To be honest, I wasn't sure I knew how one would dance to Techno music. They tried to describe it to me. When I told them I used to break dance in the eighties, they assured me it was a lot like break dancing. They insisted that I come with them one night to experience it. I politely replied, "Well, maybe one day." Inwardly, I dismissed the idea.

A few days later, during a personal time in prayer, my mind wandered to thinking about my newfound friends. The Holy Spirit said to me, "I am presenting you to them in techno color." After a moment of confusion over what the Lord was saying, I realized that God wanted me to go out with them "clubbing." So, I picked up the phone and called to accept their gracious offer. They were absolutely thrilled. A few nights later, there I was. The music was loud, the air was thick with smoke, but my companions were really happy. I even dared to venture out onto the dance floor to partake in this cultural phenomenon. I remember thinking while I was dancing, "I hope this is okay with you, Jesus. I'm doing this for you, and to reach out to these people. You told me to go. So, here I am." That night as Jesus and I left the building, I gasped to breathe the clean, fresh winter air that waited for me outside. My lungs felt as if they were going to collapse from the weight of the cigarette smoke, but inside myself resided a settling satisfaction that I had done exactly what the Lord wanted.

Meeting them on their turf went a long way. I'm sure they knew that it wasn't my scene and they never asked me to do it again. However, from that point on everything changed. One time was all it took to win their hearts. They let me into their world. They also let Jesus in. Each one of them, over the next several months, gave me a place to speak to them about my faith and relationship with Christ. They were truly open to hear what I had to say. It's as though I suddenly had a voice.

"NO ONE EVER SPOKE LIKE THIS MAN"

Jesus touched a lot of people in their area of personal need. To many He was a hero. The gospels are full of dozens of stories telling of individuals receiving healing and restoration from Jesus. Yet there were certainly many unwritten testimonies to the miraculous that came from the ministry of Christ. All the sick in entire regions were brought to Him, and He healed them all. (Matthew 4:24; 8:16; 9:35; 12:15; 14:35, 36). Fascination and fame spread throughout the countryside of Galilee as Jesus moved from place to place teaching and healing the sick. The general sentiment toward Him was, "He has done all things well. He makes both the deaf to hear and the mute to speak." (Mark 7:37)

People also listened to Jesus. His words had impact on all who heard Him, both follower and foe. After the famous Sermon on the Mount, we're told: "And so it was, when Jesus had ended these sayings, that the people were astonished at His teaching, for He taught them as one having authority, and not as the scribes." (Matthew 7:28, 29) The average person who heard the simple yet profound teachings of this new rabbi recognized something different. There was weight to His words. They felt something that stirred the depths of their hearts when He spoke. This was not their experience when hearing the homilies of the scribes. Jesus had a voice that the established spiritual leaders of the day did not.

In fact, it seems that the only ones who would not listen to Jesus were those threatened by His popularity. The Pharisees had something to lose. The people who they oppressed with their religion were finding grace, mercy and freedom because of the ministry of this Jesus of Nazareth. Consumed by jealousy and envy toward Him, they wanted nothing more than to see Jesus dead. On one occasion, crowds of people were coming to trust Jesus and saying, "Truly this is the Prophet." (John 7:31, 40) "The Pharisees heard the crowd murmuring these things concerning Him, and the Pharisees and the chief priests sent officers to take Him." (John 7:32) The officers tried, but they returned surprisingly empty handed. They couldn't do it. They had heard Jesus speak and it stopped them in their tracks. When questioned as to why the officers had not brought Jesus to them, "The officers answered, 'No man ever spoke like this Man!' Then the Pharisees answered them 'Are you also deceived?'" (John 7:45-47) These men had a direct order to arrest Jesus, but instead were themselves arrested by the words coming from His mouth. Jesus had a powerful and convincing voice!

There are probably many reasons to explain why Jesus' sayings had such a commanding influence over people. Above all, Jesus spoke what He heard His Father was saying. (John 14:10). There was *Spirit and Life* in the words that Jesus spoke. (John 6:63)

Jesus didn't tickle the intellect with empty philosophy and naïve idealism. His words traveled deeper than the brain, down into the recesses of the heart and soul. You couldn't be the same after hearing this Man. And so it was also with the early apostles who carried Jesus' imprint upon them.

The apostle Paul explained to the Corinthian believers:

> And I, brethren, when I came to you, did not come with excellence of speech or of wisdom, declaring to you the testimony of God. For I determined not to know anything among you except Jesus Christ, and Him crucified. I was with you in weakness, in fear, and in much trembling. And my speech and my preaching were not with persuasive words of human wisdom, but in demonstration of the Spirit and of power, that your faith should not be in the wisdom of men, but in the power of God. (1 Corinthians 2:1-5)

On the day of Pentecost, Peter preached his heart out to thousands of Jews in the streets. Though Peter cowered in fear the night Jesus was betrayed, something had now taken hold of this fisherman from Galilee. He had experienced failure in order to learn grace and forgiveness in a life-altering moment with the resurrected Christ. Now filled with the Holy Spirit and "clothed in power" from heaven, Peter's voice rang out loud and clear. This was the very city that crucified Christ only weeks before. None of that mattered to Peter anymore. He had found his voice. "Now when they heard this, they were cut to the heart, and said to Peter and the rest of the apostles, 'Men and brethren, what shall we do?'" (Acts 2:37)

Jesus and the church He started had a voice to their communities and culture. Jesus set the example and the early church continued being a prophetic mouthpiece. There was something authentic and irresistible about the preaching of the apostles. Like their master, the words coming off the lips of the first disciples stirred the heart and sparked faith. The public opinion of the church in Jerusalem in the first century AD was highly favorable. "Yet none of the rest dared join them, but the people esteemed them highly. And believers were increasingly added to the Lord, multitudes of both men and women." (Acts 5:13, 14) The Greek word used here to describe how the public viewed Christians means "to make great, to enlarge, to magnify, to show respect, to hold in high esteem." In those days, Christianity wasn't a four letter word. Christians had something authentic which set them apart. They had found the way to live and possessed a power that was reflected through their changed lives. People either feared this heavenly company or sought how to join them. This was not only because of their preaching.

It was told of Jesus that He was "mighty in deed and word." (Luke 24:19) The ministry of Jesus hinged upon two equally essential components. Luke, the physician, made a comment describing the writing of his gospel narrative. It was an account of "all that Jesus began both to do and teach." (Acts 1:1) Jesus had something to "show and tell." Proclamation seemed to be always partnered with demonstration. He preached the gospel of the kingdom and also demonstrated it. This "one-two punch" strategy was unstoppable. The "showing of the gospel" opens a person's heart to the "telling of the gospel." You may want to listen to the man who just opened your blind eyes or deaf ears, or raised your dead daughter, or healed your sick body, or showed kindness, or served you selflessly like no other ever had. This is what makes the good news of Jesus personal. Jesus met people's needs and got into their lives. In return, they listened to what He had to say.

Jesus touched a man with leprosy who no one else would ever touch. This leper's expectation of rejection was washed over by Jesus' love and acceptance. (Matthew 8:1-4) A similar situation occurred with the woman who had an "issue of blood." Her faith prodded her to push through a crowd that she might only touch the hem of His garment to be healed. Most likely the poor woman would not have anticipated a personal meeting with the Master. Yet Jesus made time to converse with her even though He had another pressing matter. After all, Jesus was with a man named Jairus when the interruption occurred.

Jairus stood waiting for Him to come quickly to the urgent need of his daughter lying sick, near the point of death. He might have thought, "Why has the teacher wasted precious moments to talk to this woman when my little girl needs Him most?" When suddenly word came that the girl was dead, Jairus' heart broke. With a lowered head and hopeless spirit he muttered to Jesus, "It's too late. She's gone." However, Jesus, who always seemed to see the world from a different light answered, "She's only sleeping," and continued to make the journey to Jairus' house. It was there where people learned that Jesus was more than a healer. He brought the child back to life. (Matthew 9:18-26)

Jesus had a way of getting into the space where people lived. He could relate to all manner of individuals with different experiences and backgrounds. I think of the Samaritan woman who met Jesus at a well. She was simply there to retrieve water as part of her daily routine. Since it was a Jewish man sitting near the well the Samaritan would have been shocked to have Jesus start a conversation with her. Jews hated Samaritans because of racial and religious bigotry. In addition, this Samaritan was also a woman, living in a society that had made no strides towards gender equality. Women were oppressed and considered second rate human beings, as is still the situation in many places in the world today. However, Jesus engaged this woman in dialogue, showing acceptance, and demonstrating that He was as radical in His love as He was in His teachings.

The disciples were awestruck that Jesus actually spoke to a Samaritan woman in public. They couldn't understand why He would do such a thing. Every religious bone in their bodies was crying out, "Jews have no dealings with Samaritans!" As a result of the encounter, she in turn spread the word among her people and the record shows that many Samaritans came to Jesus and believed in Him. Jesus gained a voice among these rejected people. This was undoubtedly the result of a personal and relevant interaction in the spirit of acceptance and truth.

The list is infinite. There is no way to count how many people Jesus loved back to life. Whether a leprous man, an ill woman, a dying child, a Samaritan, a prostitute, a drunk, or a tax collector named Zacchaeus, Jesus opened His heart to individuals in need of mercy. He wasn't afraid to associate Himself with "sinners," to the chagrin of His self-righteous opposition. Jesus won a place in the homes and hearts of all who experienced His unconditional love. I have heard it said, "No one cares about how much you know, until they know how much you care." This is a clue as to what gave Jesus such a prominent voice.

"Then all the tax collectors and the sinners drew near to Him to hear Him. And the Pharisees and scribes complained, saying, 'This man receives sinners and eats with them.'" (Luke 15:1-2)

"The Son of Man came eating and drinking, and they say, 'Look, a glutton and a winebibber, a friend of tax collectors and sinners!' But wisdom is justified by her children." (Matthew 11:19)

PREACHING WITHOUT WORDS

My wife and I recently had the wonderful privilege of reuniting with old friends who had sold everything they had to move to Indonesia as missionaries. It had been several years since we'd seen them. They were back to visit friends and family, as well as to raise support to return to the field. Our friends were having quite a difficult time readjusting to life in our Western culture. Our afternoon together was absolutely inspiring for Tamara and me. These people were doing it! Living on a small island, this missionary family completely assimilated into normal Indonesian life, learned the language, made meaningful relationships, and served the people selflessly. They found many creative ways to show God's love to the people. Their kindness has drawn so many into their web of love. Through acts of mercy and compassion they preach Christ, yet without words. It has to be this way. Proclaiming the gospel out loud would be the fastest way to be expelled from the country. You see, Indonesia is a Muslim nation. Christianity is outlawed.

My radical friends have to act like Christians, love like Christians, and find alternate ways of getting the heart message of the gospel to people outside of public preaching. They've had individuals come to them and ask why they are so different. In private conversations, this couple has had the opportunity to share who Jesus is and their relationship with Him.

This reminds me of a phrase I encountered while reading Wolfgang Simson's book *Houses that Change the World*. In a chapter describing the early church for the first 250 years, Simson quoted Pagan Caecilius, a contemporary of the early church, who reported that Christians were "silent in public, but chattering in corners." Direct preaching to the public masses was simply too dangerous for the church to engage in due to the resistance of Rome towards the gospel. Instead, they learned to live the message. Their lifestyle and devotion spoke to the world around them and the church grew at an astronomical rate.

Beginning in the middle of the first century, believers would never invite "pagans" to their church gatherings because of the real threat of "wolves in sheep's clothing." After the persecution released by Nero in AD 64, most churches shut their doors to the outside world. One of the early church fathers named Tertullian wrote, "We are besieged and attacked; they kept us prisoners in our own secret congregations." Like much of the church around the world today living in hostile conditions, the early church did not define their mission as "bringing unbelievers to church." They would not risk it. Their mission was to infiltrate society, like a covert operation, bringing the church out into the real world.

I don't live in a nation where Christianity is an enemy of the State, at least not yet. We have certain rights, not the least of them being freedom of speech. We can talk about Jesus all we want. Indeed, we do! There is a lot of talk going on from the church. You can hear us rant at any point night and day on radio or television. Every Sunday you'll find a church with a preacher on practically every street corner. We have magazines, books, audio cassettes, CDs, DVDs, and even motion pictures trumpeting a vast number of sermons across this land. Yet nobody is really listening. Well, I shouldn't say "nobody." Church folks have to listen. Listening to preachers is the center piece of church culture. So the books sell, and Christian entertainment is a billion dollar industry. But the world is completely out of the loop. Make no mistake about it. The church doesn't have a voice in secular culture. Society is not looking to the church for insight on what is going on in the world. They are just not interested in what the church has to say.

Perhaps part of what is working against us is that we talk too much and do very little. Are we all talk? Do people around us see Christ in the daily grind of our lives? I'm sick of Christianity just being an idea. I want to have my life look more like what Jesus modeled for us. I want to be a Christian, in the truest sense of the word. Do we need our government to oppress us to wake us up and to force us to live what we believe? Why does Christianity only seem to look right when it's under persecution? God help us! What will it take to completely reinvent Christianity in the West?

Jesus taught us that our mandate was to communicate the heart and nature of God with more than just words. He said, "Let your light so shine before men, that they may see your *good works* and glorify your Father in heaven." (Matthew 5:16, emphasis mine) Acting like Jesus is even more powerful than talking about Him. Jesus told us that if we love our enemies, do good, give without expectation of anything in return, and walk in kindness and mercy toward others, we will be "sons of the Most High." This means people will see the family resemblance. They will recognize that we look like our Father, who also is "kind to the unthankful and evil." (Luke 6:35) I believe that the general public must see a new vision of what the church truly is. Perhaps in preaching without words through heartfelt acts of kindness and love, we will regain a voice in our culture. At the very least, my neighbor will see in me a clean expression of Christ, clear of false pretense, religious arrogance, and ill motive.

Jesus cared for people and met their needs whether they decided to follow Him or not. He ministered to broken people and exercised mercy simply because it was who He was and is. He showed us what the Father in Heaven is like. I find that in my own heart I have often had a hidden agenda or "angle" when relating to unbelievers. The truth is, people can sense it when someone has ulterior motives. Whether it's a family member wanting to recruit you into the latest network marketing scheme or a creepy guy feeding you a pickup line while standing in a grocery store aisle, no one is comfortable with this scenario. People outside the walls of church can see church folk coming at them a mile away. These days I am more aware of what is working in me, and so I purposefully deflate all attempts of using "kindness" as a platform to get my little "preach" in.

I recently helped a lady who was stranded, by paying to have some gas put into her vehicle. As I was parting ways with this very thankful person, I intentionally wished her "good luck." In the past I would have talked to her about Jesus being the reason that I'm helping a poor soul like her. I didn't even want to say, "God loves you." Not that this wasn't true or a bad thing to say. I just had to get this "angle" out of me. "Good luck" is something people say (except for Christians who replace the word "luck" with "blessing" like in the phrase "pot-blessing dinner"). She would know what I meant, in that I was wishing her well. Religious language was not necessary. The act of kindness spoke for itself.

I believe Christians will once again have a voice in our culture when Jesus' teachings become our lifestyle. When people begin to see Jesus in how we relate to others without the suspicion that we want something from them, they will want to hear what we have to say. In that moment, when we have their attention we will have to know how to speak to them in a language they understand.

As Francis of Assisi said, "Preach Christ everyday. If necessary, use words."

CULTURAL LITERACY

In a previous chapter I described the Christian nature by using the analogy of an amphibian. Disciples of Jesus are able to thrive in two environments, the fellowship of believers and secular society. Like a frog on land, we can experience a new reality that wasn't imaginable in our previous life in water. However, amphibians must have a harmonious existence in both land and water to survive. Many of us have spent so long on land that we have forgotten how to swim.

We have learned to live without contact with the world. We have created an artificial environment that goes beyond the simplicity of Christian community. A culture that is not the kingdom of God, nor the kingdoms of this world, has emerged. It's called the "church culture." With its own language and customs, in many cases those who enter this culture from the outside encounter a form of culture shock. Often our friends who agree to come to "church" experience a sense of confusion, anxiety, and uncertainty, being exposed to an alien environment without adequate preparation. The cultural gap between the church and unbelievers is difficult to cross.

I believe the burden to bridge that gap must fall upon the church. Remember, we can live in both environments, but the world cannot.

The place to start in our attempt to regain our amphibious nature is to become culturally literate.

Please understand that I am not talking about changing the message of the gospel to fit the culture. The teachings of the kingdom are not user-friendly to those gripped by the spirit of the age. The message of Christ is controversial, demanding the complete sacrificial love and devotion of anyone choosing to follow Him. Jesus called His path "narrow," and many people left Him because they felt His teachings were too hard. The kingdom is a counter-culture. Making the words of Jesus more palatable by squeezing them into an acceptable cultural form will not have any power. Times of trial will quickly uncover the faulty foundation. Rather, I am describing cultural literacy.

How well can you read the culture? Do you know how to speak the language of culture? Do you really understand the person you work or go to school with? What is the cry in the heart of people who live on your street? They are not going to speak to you in the same way a believer does. Our ability to understand the worldviews of others will enable us to more effectively communicate with them. Culture is the teacher of worldviews and gives us the language with which we are able to speak.

Merriam-Webster Online Dictionary defines culture as, "the integrated pattern of human knowledge, belief, and behavior that depends on man's capacity for learning and transmitting knowledge to succeeding generations. It is the customary beliefs, social forms, and material traits of a racial, religious, or social group." Culture transmits itself from generation to generation taking slight variations in each succeeding transmission. The carriers of this transmission are language, customs, trends, philosophy, religion, heroes and people of influence.

Although as Christians we abide in a new culture called the kingdom of God, we must still know the culture that surrounds us. We are in the world, but not of it. If we are going to be effective in communicating the message of the kingdom to those who move within the limits of their culture, we must be able to speak to them in a language they can understand.

Jesus mastered the fine art of cultural literacy and spoke to the people of His day in ways that brought meaningful connection with His message. He told simple stories to illustrate the truth of the kingdom using common experiences, such as fishing or farming. The New Testament itself was written in common Greek instead of classical Greek because more people spoke it. Today we have copies of the Scripture in most of the world's languages. If God could use our own words to express His heart to us, why can't we do the same for others?

"SOME OF YOUR OWN POETS HAVE SAID"

The apostles learned well from Jesus. What aided them in establishing a voice to the people of their culture was that they knew how to adjust their language according to who was listening. An illustration of this can be found in chapter seventeen of the book of Acts. Here the apostle Paul is waiting in the city of Athens for some of his friends to join him, only to go on together to another place. Paul had a few days to kill. He could have enjoyed some "R&R" time away from his busy missionary itinerary. So there he was in the middle of this great city, when all of a sudden he noticed around him the many idols erected in every public place. The Scriptures say that, "…his spirit was provoked within him…" (Acts 17:16) The entire city was given over to idolatry. The next thing you know, Paul could be found every day in the marketplace talking to whoever happened to be there. Paul was amphibious. The culture of Athens stirred him to engage with the people in that city.

During those few days, Paul met some interesting people who considered themselves Epicurean and Stoic philosophers. Epicureans believed that the gods were not to be feared, but were merely a collection of atoms. Death was only the dissolving of the atomic structure, so not much thought was given to the idea of an afterlife. What really mattered to the Epicureans was the natural world and the pursuit of pleasure. Happiness in this life was the highest goal. [1]

The Stoic's goal was to be free from the passions of the body, which they saw as morally wrong impulses. They passively accepted everything in life as inevitable, impersonal fate. Taking control of the passions was accomplished through rigorous self-discipline and it would become the process to perfection. [2] This all sounds very familiar.

The culture we live in today is a blend of these two ancient worldviews. Epicureanism is similar to the modern worldview we have in the West. Stoicism is more an "eastern" thought, which is gaining much momentum in the postmodern circles of our culture. We live in a place where both of these philosophies have merged together. In the West we act like there is no eternity. Materialism and entertainment are the idols we worship. Science has been our religion, limiting reality to the five senses. However, in recent years a hunger has emerged to develop the sixth sense. Our culture is now much more accepting of the "spiritual" parts of life. "There are many paths to God," is the message of this pluralistic society, but in all of them God is still viewed as something impersonal and abstract. It seems to me that the culture of Athens in the first century is similar to the current Western culture. Perhaps Paul has something to teach us about how to engage this culture with the gospel.

Paul followed his new companions to a place called Mars Hill, where people participated in open debate and brought up new theories and ideas. What initially attracted these self-proclaimed philosophers to what Paul was saying was that it was something they had never heard before. Paul was bringing them entirely knew knowledge. It was so beyond anything they had ever heard of, they immediately wanted to hear more, seeking to understand it. One would think that this lack of knowledge would not be possible in a culture like ours, which has its roots in Christianity.

It's inconceivable that with churches on every street corner and preachers on TV and radio, a generation has been almost completely untouched by the gospel. My experience outside the walls these last few years has definitely confirmed this to be true. Most unbelievers really have no clue what the Bible teaches and know very little about Jesus. If we can have the courage to share with people the Jesus we know, I am convinced that just the "newness" of what they hear and see will cause people to want more.

Paul also did some homework during his stay in Athens. He spent time passing through the objects of worship in the city, considering and familiarizing himself with their religious culture. (Acts 17:23) As he was doing this, he encountered an altar with this inscription: "To the unknown God." The people of Athens included in their worship a deity they did not know. Paul had discovered an inroad into the hearts and minds of the Athenians.

Could it be that there are people in our life who are longing to connect with God but just don't know how? Are there things about our culture that provide a springboard for the gospel to be preached and demonstrated? I believe that God has provided exit doors in every culture around the world. These are subtle passage ways to finding God, where culture and the kingdom intersect. We, as amphibious Christians, can possess the insight to locate these portals. They are simply entry points that provide opportunity for us to share Christ.

Often these entry points are found in the artistic parts of culture. Paul understood this when he quoted the Greek poets in his message that day on Mars Hill; "As also some of your own poets have said, 'for we are also His offspring.'" (Acts 17:28) It's interesting to note that Paul doesn't quote the Bible once in his appeal to the Athenians. They would not have had any point of reference in regards to the Hebrew Scriptures. Paul must have researched the writings of the Greek philosophers and poets in order to be able to speak to that culture. Paul used their own trusted sources as a basis of presenting the gospel of Jesus to these people.

Who are the trusted sources of our culture? Stephen Spielberg, John Lennon, Sting, Michael Jordan, Bono, Eminem, Jennifer Lopez, Larry and Andy Wachowski, J.R.R. Tolkien, and George Lucas, to name only a few. These are the poets, musicians, artists and storytellers of our time. Whether you agree with it or not, these are the trusted sources of our culture. Hidden in the songs, books, movies, sporting events, and cultural phenomena are gateways. Thoughts, ideas, statements, pictures, and metaphors that line up with truth in the gospel message are waiting to be interpreted and proclaimed. The followers of Jesus are the interpreters of the divine revelation that God is speaking through culture. Without us, the truth lies there undiscovered. The precious goes unnoticed in the heap of the worthless.

Paul's approach on Mars Hill is also very helpful for believers who are living in a postmodern world which celebrates cultural diversity and possesses a global awareness. Paul presents God in an all encompassing way. He's not merely the God of a specific religion or ethnicity; the true and living God is the God of all people. Christians these days are often viewed as being narrow-minded and exclusive. There are inaccurate perceptions that Christianity is a Western religion. You can see it in arenas of global conflict, as in the fight between the Muslim Arab world and "Christian" America. However, Jesus has many followers in the Third World and is not restricted to a certain race or tribe of people.

Here are a few of the phrases spoken by Paul that day on Mars Hill:

> God who made *the world and everything in it*...Lord of heaven and earth...He gives to *all*...made *from one blood every nation*...has determined their pre-appointed times and the boundaries of their dwellings, so that they should seek the Lord, in the hope that they might grope for Him and find Him, though *He is not far from each one of us*...*We are the offspring* of God. (Acts 17:24-29, emphases mine)

Paul did not condemn the Athenians for their errors in theology. He did not limit God's involvement to a small group of "chosen" ones. He also debunked the understanding that God could be contained in buildings by his statement, *"Nor does He dwell in temples made with hands."* Paul preached a God who was outside the building. God is who He is and our finite minds cannot even scratch the surface of uncovering His immensity. Paul's God was universal and near to every human heart on the planet. He taught that God was the one who had chosen the time periods and nations into which people were to be born. Every human being exists for the same purpose: to search and grope for God. Anyone, anywhere can find Him if they allow their heart to open and respond to the stimulus God has placed in creation. Followers of Christ need only to recognize the desire in people to connect with their Creator and help them interpret the signs already found in human consciousness as expressed through art and literature. Jesus can be seen outside the walls of the organized church.

PARTICIPATE IN THE CULTURE

It really doesn't take much to become culturally literate and learn the language of the culture. Years of study and research are not required. I am not asking you to buy a stack of music CDs or rent a new movie release every night. All it takes is involvement. If believers can commit themselves to relationship with people, reading the culture becomes natural. Culture is written on people. I always ask the people that I'm getting to know what kind of music they like or what their favorite movie is, and why. What do people like to do for fun or where do they go to relax? Asking questions, being truly interested in people, and enjoying those people is all the research needed to become culturally literate. Are you willing to participate?

Do more than just tolerate our culture. Do more than accept it or be educated about it. Being amphibious means participating in the culture. This can mean so many things. Buy your neighbor a Christmas gift. Take a friend to the movies. Have your coworkers from the office over for a Super Bowl party. Maybe your brother-in-law wants to take you fishing next weekend. Go and enjoy yourself. Be with people. Engage in what people do in the culture that you live in. Take time to build lasting and meaningful friendships. Do you have the time?

Often we can't afford the time to participate in cultural activity or build relationships with our neighbor because we are too busy "doing church." The church sub-culture can be a very hectic place. In addition to the Sunday morning, Sunday evening and Wednesday night services, anyone wanting to be involved with the church will have to commit to one or two more evenings a week. Whether you go to choir practice, a deacons' meeting, a ladies' prayer gathering, Bible study, home group, or men's breakfast, the schedule is quickly filled. When do we have a moment for people who don't know Jesus? When do we have a free night to engage the culture?

I don't believe that being busy is necessarily wrong. I think busyness without fruitfulness is a curse. It is the curse of the fall spoken to Adam so long ago. We see this curse in the world and even in the church. We work and work, but have little to no results for our labor. I am convinced that the most fruitful investment you could ever make into the kingdom is to spend time with unbelieving friends, doing the things that they love to do.

> For though I am free from all men, I have made myself a servant to all, that I might win the more; and to the Jews I became as a Jew, that I might win Jews; to those who are under the law, as under the law, that I might win those who are under the law; to those who are without law, as without law (not being without law toward God, but under law toward Christ), that I might win those who are without law; to the weak I became weak, that I might win the weak. I have become all things to all men, that I might by

all means save some. Now this I do for the gospel's sake, that I might be partaker of it with you. (1 Corinthians 9:19-23)

Now when Peter had come to Antioch, I withstood him to his face, because he was to be blamed; for before certain men came from James, he would eat with the Gentiles; but when they came, he withdrew and separated himself, fearing those who were of the circumcision. And the rest of the Jews also played the hypocrite with him, so that even Barnabas was carried away with their hypocrisy. But when I saw that they were not straightforward about the truth of the gospel, I said to Peter before them all, "If you, being a Jew, live in the manner of Gentiles and not as the Jews, why do you compel Gentiles to live as Jews?" (Galatians 2: 11-14)

WHY MAKE ENEMIES?

Criticism and judgment never win the heart of a person. Attacking cultural customs or trends is coming against the beliefs and values of people. For example, if you are not personally into getting every part of your body pierced, that is fine. Please consider refraining from sharing your distaste for this publicly, especially because someone around you is most likely body pierced. What is the point of closing the door on anyone simply because they are different?

Some may feel that they are compromising if they don't visibly show their disapproval of sin. How quickly we forget our former habitat.

Sinners sin! This is what they do. This is what we were doing before the metamorphosis, and sin is what we are still capable of when we're not ourselves. Why is it so shocking for us to see sin in the lives of the people around us? The hypocrisy is evident as the church rants and raves about the sexual immorality and devaluing of family in our society, only for the world to hear about the secret sins of preachers on TV and the higher divorce rate among church people than non-church people. *"Judge not, that you be not judged."* (Matthew 7:1)

Jesus never exposed the sin of the sinners. He loved them and received them as friends. His kindness led people to want to be better. I love the story of the woman caught in adultery. When her religious accusers cast her down at the feet of Jesus to be condemned, Jesus responded with the statement, "Let you who have not sinned cast the first stone." One by one the stones fell to the ground as each accuser left the scene. Jesus and the woman were alone. He asked her if there was anyone left to condemn her. When she realized they were all gone, Jesus spoke these kind words to her, "Neither will I condemn you. Go and sin no more." I'm convinced that this woman's life did change. The kindness and mercy that Jesus showed her made her want to be a better person. She was forgiven by the only One who had the right to cast the stone. It is, "the goodness of God that leads you to repentance." (Romans 2:4)

Our message to the culture should be "reconciliation." (2 Corinthians 5:18-21) God is bringing people to Him through the death and resurrection of Jesus. He wants relationship restored. He is freely giving forgiveness to this world. Why are we presenting an image of Jesus that is more about rejection than reconciliation? When we distance ourselves from sinners, we are sending them the message that God is doing the same thing. This is another reason why the church has no real voice in the culture. Jesus has been misrepresented for too long.

In one of the first house churches that we started, there was a gay man who came for a period of maybe six months. He struggled with this all his life, hating himself for it. He had grown up in a religious family and had always felt extremely condemned, especially when he finally decided to "come out of the closet." He first came with all his guards up. I could see that he was hurt, but desperately wanting to connect with God. To my knowledge, we never made him feel like a castaway. I would greet him the same way I greeted everyone else, with a hug. He finally decided to leave our group because "we were too straight for him." He felt a need to surround himself with other homosexuals. I was sorry that he left, but I was glad he was rejecting us and not the other way around. I can only hope seeds of God's love were planted in his heart from that short period of time with us.

THE REVEALER OF SECRETS

Daniel is becoming one of my very favorite characters in the Scriptures. I want to be a man like Daniel. He was only a teenager when he was taken and deported to Babylon in 605 BC. King Nebuchadnezzar rose to power that year, defeating Egypt and expanding the nation of Babylon into a world empire. Daniel was among a small group of early exiles from Judah (including his three friends; Daniel 1:1, 7) brought back to Babylon to serve the king in governing his large empire. Daniel spent the next sixty years of his life in this foreign culture.

Daniel and three of his friends were placed into a three-year training program designed to erase their previous cultural identity and completely immerse them in Babylonian society. They were even given new Babylonian names. All that Daniel knew and had grown up with was gone. There were no cultural or religious props for him to lean upon from his Jewish upbringing. He would have to stand strong in his faith while in a pagan culture, depending solely on his own relationship with God.

Those first exiles of Judah would have felt utterly alone. In fact, they had no temple or public gathering to depend on. They would seek each other out to huddle together in small groups and encourage one another in the faith. Yet in spite of this total saturation in the Babylonian way of life, Daniel thrived and maintained serious integrity and deep faithfulness to God. Although Daniel was far from home and from all external reinforcement of the faith of his youth, he assimilated into his new culture without compromising his convictions. He continued steadfastly in daily prayer, trusted God in the face of persecution, and refrained from indulging in the excess of that culture. God blessed Daniel and he excelled. "As for these four young men, God gave them knowledge and skill in all literature and wisdom; and Daniel had understanding in all visions and dreams." (Daniel 1:17)

Daniel and his friends became culturally literate. God gave them the ability to understand Babylonian philosophy and literature. He had placed them in a position to impact the most powerful man and nation in the world. These young leaders could speak the language. They knew the history and understood the issues. This was a work of God in them and He was going to give them a voice to speak. Not only did Daniel know Babylonia, he knew the mysteries of God. Daniel possessed the divine ability to understand visions and interpret dreams. Cultural literacy with supernatural revelation—what a powerful combination!

These early exiles had a profound impact on King Nebuchadnezzar. This was a man who ruled the world. He was untouchable and consumed with arrogance. This king demanded that all men worship him as a god. In the end, largely due to Daniel and his friends, the king's testimony was, "Now I, Nebuchadnezzar, praise and extol and honor the King of heaven, all of whose works are truth, and His ways justice. And those who walk in pride He is able to put down." (Daniel 4:37)

Daniel's first encounter with Nebuchadnezzar set the pace for his successful career and relationship to the king. In the second year of his reign, the king had a dream. This dream was extremely troubling to Nebuchadnezzar. He knew it was more than just an overactive subconscious. Something or someone from beyond the world of men was trying to communicate with him. He knew the vision in his dream was significantly prophetic. However, he couldn't understand it. It was a mystery that needed interpretation. Who could accurately reveal this secret?

The king called upon all the magicians, astrologers, sorcerers, and wise men in his kingdom. His spirit was anxious to know the meaning of his dream; however, he wanted something real. Nebuchadnezzar had come to this point where he had lost faith in the reliability and authenticity of those claiming to understand the spirit world. This dream was important and the king needed some answers. He was not going to settle for some empty form of wisdom. He accused his wise men of speaking lies in the past, projecting an image that they could reveal mysteries, but in fact were only guessing and hoping the scenario would turn in their favor. The king was finally calling their bluff. He was sick and tired of the guise of spiritual understanding that these gurus claimed to possess. Their words were like shifting shadows, with no substance at all. The longing of the king, in response to this powerful spiritual experience was, "Give me something real that will bring peace to my heart. I want the truth!"

As a result, Nebuchadnezzar refused to tell his wise men what the dream actually was. He commanded that they, through supernatural revelation, tell him what he saw in the vision, and then proceed to interpret it. Whoever claimed to be a "spiritual guide" and yet could not tell the king his dream would be sentenced to a brutal death. The magicians begged the king to tell them the dream. Only then could they interpret it for him. They claimed that no man would be able to tell the king his own dream. They insisted that only a god could do this and that the gods didn't walk among men. King Nebuchadnezzar was furious at their answer and the decree went forth to destroy all wise men in Babylon.

Daniel heard word of this decree even as the first wise men were being killed. He knew that he and his three friends would also be numbered among this outlawed band of spiritualists. Daniel quickly responded by making a request to the king's captain to ask Nebuchadnezzar for some time. Daniel would tell the king his dream. That very night Daniel and his companions called out to God for mercy, that He would spare their lives and the lives of all the wise men of Babylon. "Then the secret was revealed to Daniel in a night vision." (Daniel 2:19)

The next day Daniel interceded for the wise men before the king and proceeded to tell the dream and explain its meaning. The Scriptures tell us:

> Then King Nebuchadnezzar fell on his face, prostrate before
> Daniel, and commanded that they should present an offering

and incense to him. The king answered Daniel, and said, "Truly, your God is the God of gods, the Lord of kings, and a revealer of secrets, since you could reveal this secret." Then the king promoted Daniel and gave him many great gifts; and made him ruler over the whole province of Babylon, and chief administrator over all the wise men of Babylon. (Daniel 2:46-48)

"POST"-POSTMODERN

I believe this story may give us a hint as to what the days ahead will look like. Postmodernism is an intermediate ideology for our culture. In chapter five I told you that I had some idea as to what the "post"-postmodern world may be. Where does postmodernism take us? Not unlike King Nebuchadnezzar, the postmodern generation is hungry to know the truth in a personal way. We want answers to the unsettling questions of life. Unfortunately, most are not looking for these answers to come from the church. They feel as though Christianity has failed and are quite eager to look elsewhere. As a result, all doors of spirituality are being opened and all options are being tested. Experimentation with the supernatural in every form has become a benchmark of postmodern society. As people create a personal history in the pursuit of "spirituality," I believe their paths will inexorably lead toward something more.

I truly believe that as a culture we will arrive at the same place Nebuchadnezzar did. As individuals continue to navigate the terrain of spirituality in search of a place to settle, no such place will be found. The search will go on endlessly until a certain point is reached. That point is the realization that nobody has the answers. We have been fed empty words. I believe our culture is going to lose faith in those who claim to be spiritually astute. Through a trail of lies and hollow promises given to us by the spiritualists, New Age gurus, mediums, fortune-tellers, psychics, and the gamut of enlightened souls that bid us continually to trust their guidance, our society will grow in scepticism of our modern day wise men. Western society is racing to discover how to be happy and spiritually fulfilled. We may just be some of the most miserable people on the planet. When the pursuit of spirituality leaves many still wanting, the scene will be set for the emergence of Daniel.

The remarkable thing about that time will be that people will still be experiencing the supernatural. The modern era fooled us into thinking that the spiritual world did not exist. Postmodernism has given us the permission to seek out that world. What happens when spiritually-minded people exhaust every possibility of finding peace within? What happens when the public opinion of all "wise men" changes to resentment and cynicism because they have no real answers? All the while, spiritual encounters will increase in frequency and magnitude. However, no one will know what it all means. Our culture will need a true interpreter and revealer of secrets. This will be the hour for Daniel, true men and women who know God and are able to speak on His behalf. The followers of Christ will once again find themselves in the world, with the revelation and authority to be able to speak to it. We will have a voice!

DANIELS—TAKE YOUR PLACE

Daniel's ministry continued as kings came and went, and kingdoms

244

rose and fell. It was Daniel who interpreted the infamous "handwriting on the wall," saying that God was going to bring down the Babylonian empire in the reign of King Belshazzar, Nebuchadnezzar's son. (Daniel 5) Daniel remained in his place of influence even after the Medes took control of Babylon under King Darius, and also during the reign of Cyrus, the Persian king. (Daniel 6:28) His place in God was unshakeable and unmovable. He became a steady and proven voice for God to the kingdoms of the world, discerning the times and revealing mysteries of the divine will.

The Hebrew children had come to this place in history to fulfill a most critical role. Major world events of their time would also cast a shadow into the future, culminating at the end of the age, and Daniel would be a main revealer of these mysteries. The Babylonian exilic period foreshadows the events of the Second Coming of Christ. This is why the book of Revelation is so closely associated with the book of Daniel. Daniel represents a generation that carries the divine mandate to be a voice to kings and nations in a time when God is bringing judgment on the world. I believe that Daniel's message is as relevant today to our generation as it was back then. God is beginning to move modern day Daniels into the world to take their place in destiny.

Like Daniel, these early exiles will excel in the culture of our times, occupying positions of influence throughout society. They are exiles of the church, and God has moved them outside the walls. They will be prophets in the marketplace. God needs His people in all sectors of society, where they will be able to interpret to the people the messages God is sending them.

Much has to happen before this becomes a reality. However, rest assured, it will come to pass. The church will regain its voice to the world, but not as it exists today. Some major changes are going to happen to the church before God can use His people to be prophets to our culture and society. These changes have to be nothing short of radical and extreme: an exile! Daniel and his friends would have never been able to impact the world the way they did if they were still back in Judah. For these young men, life as they knew it was over. They had to leave it all behind, and never look back.

Daniel was a displaced person. He would be too "Babylonian" for those back home, and yet would have a very distinguishable lifestyle from the other Babylonian young men of his time. As it was then, so it is now.

There is an exile taking place today. Some have left early, while others are still to come. This new breed of believers are exiting the homeland of the "institutional church" and finding themselves submerged in a new form of Babylon. Yet we don't truly belong to either. We are learning a foreign culture and God is preparing us for our prophetic mission. Cultural literacy and divine interpretation will be the tools of our effectiveness as a mouthpiece for the true, living God. Jesus has left the building. There are some who have already joined Him and yes, many more will. In the following chapters you will hear more about this as we come to the question you may have been asking all along, "Do I have to leave the building too?"

NOTES:
1. "Epicureanism." *Encyclopædia Britannica* (Encyclopædia Britannica Premium Service, 2005).
2. "Stoicism." *Encyclopædia Britannica* (Encyclopædia Britannica Premium Service, 2005)

CHAPTER SIXTEEN

A MAN AMONG THE EXILES

The Exile was an event that happened almost 2600 years ago. The year was 586 BC when the Babylonian armies under the leadership of King Nebuchadnezzar utterly destroyed Solomon's temple and the entire city of Jerusalem. Many died, but those who survived the attack were carried away captive to the city of Babylon, along with the treasures of Solomon's palace and the temple. It was a judgment against the southern kingdom of Judah and the holy city. God had warned them, but they did not take heed.

In all my years of walking with God, I have never been inspired to study this part of Israel's history. I can't remember hearing any teaching about the Exile, at least any of which seemed to impact me in a relevant way. It was while I was reading the account of Daniel, chapter two, that my interest in this time period was piqued.

Daniel had heard of the terrible decree that came from the king to destroy all the wise men of the empire. As we saw in the last chapter, Daniel had received the meaning to Nebuchadnezzar's dream and he desperately desired to talk to the king before any more deaths were administered. Daniel approached Arioch, the one whom the king appointed to carry out the executions, and requested that he be taken to the king. "Then Arioch quickly brought Daniel before the king, and said thus to him, 'I have found a man of the exiles of Judah, who will make known to the king the interpretation.'" (Daniel 2:25)

This is the phrase that leapt out at me, "a man among the captives of Judah." Instantly a forcible thought rose from my heart into the forefront of my mind. "I am an exile of Judah!" God was showing me how this whole event of the Exile was happening again in a new time and different way. At present, compared to the masses of people still attending church, there have been a smaller number of believers who have left the building. Judah represents the organized Christian church and the first exiles are those who have left for various reasons. These are not people who have lost their faith. Rather, it is because of a holy dissatisfaction that they have risked everything to find God outside the walls of formalized worship. They have stopped "going" to church to learn what it means to "be" the church. This has been my experience and that of others I know.

We are early exiles, and I am convinced that this is only the tip of the iceberg. Many more will leave the building and I hope you are beginning to consider the possibility that this is a move of God. We are learning the ways of a global culture, the modern Babylon. God has a purpose in this. This truly was a special time in history, a prophetic glimpse of future generations when God would deal severely and lovingly with His people.

The Exile is one of the hot spots, historically and prophetically, in all of Israel's history with God. It was so significant that God assigned many prophets to speak His word to zero in on this specific event. The Old Testament prophetic writings of Zephaniah, Nahum, Habakkuk, Joel, Jeremiah, Ezekiel, Obadiah, and Daniel are all centered on the exile of Judah. God is trying to tell us something through this ancient episode.

What many believers may not know is that the Exile did not happen in one fell swoop, but over a period of nineteen years, with three distinct deportations. First of all, a small group of captives were taken in 605 BC. Eight years later 10,000 more were deported in 597 BC, with the third, largest, and final capture happening in 586 BC. We will refer to these latter two shortly, but for now I would like you to notice important aspects of the earliest exile where those taken captive were primarily from the younger generation in Judah.

Men who showed great potential and skill to be trained in the ways of Babylon were taken to fill bureaucratic positions of administration and influence. Of course, as you already know, Daniel was among this band of early exiles. Like the emerging generations of our times, Daniel and his friends left behind the religious landscape of their childhood to be completely immersed in Babylonian philosophy. They were literally shaped by the global culture of their day, and in a moment of providence, seized their destiny.

These unique generations don't come our way very often. Whether it's Joseph, locked in an Egyptian dungeon; David, hiding for his life in a desert cave; Daniel, forced to deny his heritage to become Babylonian; or Generation X, jaded and feeling aborted and abandoned by society; God has His way of using tribulation and heartache to prepare and position His revolutionaries. In God's perfect time all of these have risen to become a voice to the culture of their world.

JUDGMENT BEGINS AT THE HOUSE OF GOD

In the days to come, our nation will depend on us to interpret and proclaim God's wisdom when judgment is being poured out. King Nebuchadnezzar needed Daniel and so did the kings who succeeded him. Daniel revealed the mysteries of God to a pagan world in times of great confusion and global crisis. How will believers have this kind of influence once again in our own culture with the kind of reputation that Christianity has right now? It's been bad for a long time. Even the great human rights leader Gandhi, who was Hindu, once said, "I would be a Christian if it weren't for Christians." He too had an unfavorable experience with the church.

Our society is going to have to meet followers of Jesus who don't "go to church." We will have to shed that old skin, the stigma and reproach that hinder our impact. Disciples of Christ will need to take on a whole new form to slip through by stealth into crucial sectors of society. We must become Babylonians. We will be like them, yet with a difference. They will see Jesus in us!

Before God's people can take their prophetic role in Western society, our own Babylonia, a large-scale purging must take place in the church. Judgment is coming to the West, of that I am now certain. However, God's mercy will desire to provide these First World countries with authentic expressions of Christ within their borders. These will be people who are passionately in love with Jesus. They will speak God's heart and demonstrate his character, acting as safe houses in tumultuous times. The church is not ready for this. In fact, before judgment comes to the culture, it must first pass through the church.

"For the time has come for judgment to begin at the house of God; and if it begins with us first, what will be the end of those who do not obey the gospel of God?" (1 Peter 4:17) This verse is taken from a passage where Peter encouraged believers to endure suffering for God's glory. He encourages us to not think it strange for believers to go through trials, but that this is part of what it means to follow Christ.

In contrast to what many seem to be teaching today, there is a suffering that is "according to the will of God." (1 Peter 4:19) Peter clarifies that this kind of hardship is not a consequence of doing evil, but a genuine testing of that Christian's experience. Into this topic he introduces the idea that mild judgment begins with the church, finishing with harsher judgment on those who are disobedient to the gospel.

Judgment has very negative connotations for us. Discipline may be a more appropriate word to use here. We must understand that God is committed to making us better, conforming us to the very image of Christ. He also wants to remove all other distractions and destructive passions that keep us from knowing Him intimately. God is going to use hardship to help shape His people into a clear expression of Jesus to our culture. Remember that it is God's dream to have His sons and daughters represent Jesus, to incarnate His glory, and cause the knowledge of that glory to cover the earth. As Moses learned so long ago, God is concerned about His reputation throughout the nations of the earth.

Judgment must begin at the house of God and from there go outward. If this order isn't followed, then there will be no clear voice and true expression of Christ to the culture in the terrible day of the Lord. The church wouldn't be ready and confusion would reign supreme. Who would speak for God? In those days the knowledge of God will be worth more than gold, and spiritual understanding the most sought after commodity.

The Exile of Judah was a judgment that came to cleanse the people in order to make them a witness to the surrounding pagan nations of the glory of God. This was always meant to be. However, instead of being a people that stood apart from all other peoples, Judah was no different.

It was God's love and faithfulness to His people, and a commitment to finish His work in them, that caused Him to send a prophet to warn and woo fallen Judah. This servant of God was later called the "Weeping Prophet," the man Jeremiah.

"YOU TRUST IN LYING WORDS"

From a very early age Jeremiah was called to prophecy to his nation of Judah. His message became a burden to him, only because no one would listen to the caution he brought, seeing what was coming in the near future. Jeremiah was commanded by God not to marry or have children to illustrate the message that judgment was pending and that the next generation would be taken away. He began to prophecy around 626 BC, giving the people of his land forty years to respond before the final deportation of 586 BC would end their once peaceful existence. Josiah was a good king when Jeremiah began his ministry. However, Jeremiah would live on to survive three succeeding kings (Jehoiakim, Jehoiachin, and Zedekiah) whose political folly led to the destruction of their society. All of it could have been avoided if they had listened to the words of Jeremiah. The fact that the entire nation ignored his warnings caused the prophet great pain for the majority of his life.

One of the first public messages Jeremiah proclaimed was on the day God instructed him to stand in the gate of the Lord's house, the temple of Solomon, and give the word of the Lord to the people entering.

Thus says the LORD of hosts, the God of Israel: "Amend your ways and your doings, and I will cause you to dwell in this place. *Do not trust in these lying words*, saying, 'The temple of the LORD,

the temple of the LORD, the temple of the LORD are these.'"
(Jeremiah 7:3, 4, emphasis mine)

The people of Jerusalem had put their trust in the temple to save them. Over a hundred years in the past, God made a promise to protect the city from destruction by the Assyrian king. (Isaiah 37:6, 7, 29) However, the times had changed and God was quite ready to level the city and its temple if the people would not amend their ways. It's often a common practice to pick Scriptures or stand on promises that support our position with little thought to context. There are other verses that we may not feel comfortable with and try to ignore, even though they may be exactly what God is revealing in the season we are in. What is God saying now? Are we preaching a time of peace when God is saying, "amend your ways"?

The citizens of Jerusalem had a false sense of security. They believed that they were safe because of their connection to the temple. They couldn't fathom that the religious structure, which God at one time instituted, could ever be abandoned by Him. They trusted in a deceptive idea. This was an idea that was proclaimed by the rulers, priests, and false prophets of their day. Only Jeremiah had what was clearly a "negative" message. Yet he stood alone as the only one speaking the truth. In verse eight of the same chapter, Jeremiah repeated once again:

Behold, you trust in lying words that cannot profit. Will you steal, murder, commit adultery, swear falsely, burn incense to Baal, and walk after gods whom you do not know, and then come and stand before Me in this house which is called by My name, and say, "We are delivered to do all these abominations"? (Jeremiah 7:8-10)

God's people were living sinful lifestyles no different from the pagan nations around them. Yet because they were "the chosen people" and they trusted in the temple to save them, they felt impenetrable to the dealings of God. This is much like the notion that we can live like the devil Monday to Saturday as long as we go to church on Sunday. To many this is an obvious absurdity, but nonetheless this type of attitude is prevalent in church culture. Most churchgoers do believe they have a certain degree of immunity to judgment simply because they go to church. We have a misguided faith in our connection to the church as an institution. We feel safe behind its four walls. Perhaps this security is in our denominational affiliation, or in adherence to certain theological positions, or just due to the fact that in some way we are associated with "Christianity." Who would dare to imagine that God would ever dismantle the church as we know it? It's been here for so long. Nothing could sink this ship.

Biblical history tells a different story. It seems as though God has no trouble forsaking an old form to move onto something new, even if it was He who established it in the first place. In Jeremiah 7, God brings to the peoples memory an example from their past, where God left the building. "But go now to My place which was in Shiloh, where I set My name at the first, and see what I did to it because of the wickedness of My people Israel." (Jeremiah 7:12) God is saying, "I've done this before and I can do it again!"

There is precedence in history for the reality that God may destroy something He started if it has lost its original purpose. The people of Jeremiah's day were back in the same spot they were in when the tabernacle of Moses resided in Shiloh. They were putting their trust in the temple of Solomon, much like they once did at Shiloh, by trusting in the ark of the covenant. This precipitated the need for the tabernacle of David, as we already discovered. We learned that the structure that was designed to facilitate worship became the object of worship. People had faith in their systems and lost intimacy with God. The same thing is happening again. Don't believe for a second that God would hesitate to bring down this very system we call "church." It seems that God has no "sacred cows." He is not gripped by nostalgia. Remember Shiloh!

In addition to the abominations already stated above, the people were throwing their own children into the fire to worship the heathen god Molech. (Jeremiah 7:30, 31) This was something that not only did God command them not to do, but it never even "entered His heart." Anything we do in the name of "worship" that sacrifices our children is not God's idea. Perhaps our children have been the greatest casualties of religion, and preacher's kids have been the most unfortunate of all. Any form of church that doesn't embrace children is not moving in the current of God's heart. Jesus was greatly displeased by his disciples intolerance of little ones. He said, "Let the little children come to Me, and do not forbid them; for of such is the kingdom of God." (Mark 10: 14)

God showed Jeremiah's generation how they were expected to amend their ways. Much of it had to do with changing their doings concerning the poor. The Lord commanded the people of Jerusalem "not to oppress the stranger, the fatherless, and the widow" and to "not shed innocent blood." (Jeremiah 7:6) As we know, the core of the sin of Sodom was their gross neglect of the poor. It was Ezekiel who revealed it to us. He too prophesied during the very same time period as Jeremiah. Jeremiah was in Jerusalem, while Ezekiel prophesied from Babylon, taken as an early exile. Ezekiel rebuked Judah for being worse than Sodom. (Ezekiel 16:48) It is clear that this issue of how we treat the poor fueled not only the destruction of Sodom, but of Jerusalem as well. How can we think here in the West that we are not culpable?

History does repeat itself. God is gracious to reveal to us what He has done in the past in order to change the outcome of our future. Seventy years after the ultimate destruction of Jerusalem and exile of its inhabitants, God brought His people back. They rebuilt the city and a new temple. Everything was wonderful for awhile. However, as time lapsed, Israel once again slid back into old habits and forgot the goodness of God. This second rebuilt temple was the structure that Jesus walked into over five hundred years later. It was the same as it was in Jeremiah's day. The people had lost their relationship with the God of Israel. Jesus quoted Jeremiah 7:11 upon entering the temple, saying: "Has this house, which is called by My name become a den of thieves?" It was happening again: first Shiloh, then Solomon's temple and now the second temple. What did God do about it? He did what He has always done. In AD 70, Prince Titus of Rome attacked the city of Jerusalem and destroyed it, along with the temple. But God would never dismantle our organized churches! Don't be so sure.

> Then Jesus went out and departed from the temple [Note: Jesus left the building], and His disciples came up to show Him the buildings of the temple. And Jesus said to them, "Do you not see all these things? Assuredly, I say to you, not one stone shall be left here upon another, that shall not be thrown down." (Matthew 24:1-2)

CHAPTER SEVENTEEN

Do I Have To Leave The Building Too?

"Do I have to leave the building too?" Until now I have been open and honest with you about my own personal journey outside the walls. I hope that I've adequately described some of the shared characteristics of my generation, with an understanding that my experience in leaving organized church is more common than one may think. I have tried to demonstrate from Scripture that there is precedence for God to move outside the defined boundaries of previous structures of worship in order to set the stage for something new. Rather than focus on what is wrong with the church, I felt it was more constructive to paint a picture of what was right about the church that Jesus started. Hopefully, as a reader, you have come to a place of peace with those who have left the church and are open to the probability that God is leading such individuals. Furthermore, I trust this book has helped to stir a longing in your heart for more of Jesus and less of religion.

Now we come to the climax, the question you've most likely been asking all along. Where is he going with this? Is this movement of Christians out of organized Christianity something happening to a few or will it escalate full scale, right across the church in the West? Do I have to leave the building too? Jeremiah has more to say about this. We must look back to see what lies ahead.

It is my belief that the role of the church is to be a prophetic voice to the culture. Jesus and the early church had a voice and we examined some of the reasons for this. However, I don't see the church in the West walking with the same influence and authority. There may be a few individuals who do, but the church as a whole has lost its place in our society as a reliable conscience of divine revelation.

Throughout history we've seen the Almighty bring judgment to nations, hoping to arouse a national turning to God, but not before cleansing His own people first. In order to present a clear expression of His heart to the people of a secular society that will soon come under the severity of God's dealings, judgment must begin with the church. The exiles of Judah were such a people in the land of Babylon. Daniel serves as an icon, or symbol, of the role the church must have in culture, especially as we approach the end of the age. However, before the administration of judgment had come to Jerusalem, there was one man who stood alone to bring God's word to the people of Judah.

WHY WILL YOU DIE?

Jeremiah called his people to repentance in hopes that the judgment being spoken against Jerusalem might be averted. In the last chapter we discovered the nature of the grievance that God had against His people. Although the message of repentance is often difficult for humans to receive, especially from the mouth of a holy prophet, there was something else that Jeremiah proclaimed that made his message a "hard pill to swallow" for the inhabitants of Jerusalem.

King Nebuchadnezzar was the most powerful man in the world. He had conquered many nations and his empire grew quickly and became vast. To the citizens of Judah, his was the new face of evil. He was a godless pagan, driven by conquest and consumed by pride and self exaltation. He was an enemy to the people of God. All the prophets in Judah were united in their message to Jerusalem. They proclaimed that God's people must stand and fight against Nebuchadnezzar. They assured the people that God was with them to strengthen their militant resistance to the Babylonian king. One prophet named Hananiah was even so bold as to announce, "Thus says the LORD: 'Even so I will break the yoke of Nebuchadnezzar king of Babylon from the neck of all nations within the space of two full years.'" (Jeremiah 28:11)

How encouraging and inspiring this message would have been to the population of Judah. The king of Judah and people of Jerusalem believed the unanimous word of these prophets and positioned themselves to fight against Nebuchadnezzar. Unfortunately, they all prophesied a lie. Jeremiah's council was completely opposite to this popular and prevailing view of the situation. Jeremiah's message was too absurd to believe and yet, as they soon discovered, it was the truth.

The twenty-seventh chapter of Jeremiah contains this strange prophetic word to Jerusalem. God's perspective on King Nebuchadnezzar is shocking! This is what God said.

"I have made the earth, the man and the beast that are on the ground, by My great power and by My outstretched arm, and have given it to whom it seemed proper to Me. And now I have given all these lands into the hand of Nebuchadnezzar the king of Babylon, My servant." (See verses 5-6.) Imagine how difficult it would have been for Jeremiah's audience to hear God call this wicked man "My servant." God had given the entire world to the Babylonian king. However, it was for a season, and then Babylon itself would come under judgment. "So all nations shall serve him and his son and his son's son, until the time of his land comes; and then many nations and great kings shall make him serve them." (See verse 7)

The message goes on to instruct God's people in responding to His servant Nebuchadnezzar.

> And it shall be, that the nation and kingdom which will not serve Nebuchadnezzar the king of Babylon, and which will not put its neck under the yoke of the king of Babylon, that nation I will punish, says the LORD, with the sword, the famine, and the pestilence, until I have consumed them by his hand. (verse 8)

God promised the people of any land that if they submitted to and served Nebuchadnezzar, they would be allowed to dwell safely in their own land. This included Judah and the people of Jerusalem.

However, the false prophets continued to incite the people to resist, saying, "You shall not serve the king of Babylon." God warned them through Jeremiah by saying,

> "Therefore, do not listen to your prophets, your diviners, your dreamers, your soothsayers, or your sorcerers…for they prophecy a lie to you, to remove you far from your land; and I will drive you out, and you will perish…for I have not sent them…they prophecy a lie in My name." (verses 9, 10, 15a)

Who would you believe? Everybody was insisting that resistance was God's will, and only one prophet spoke otherwise. "Victory" is always a more tantalizing message to receive than submission and apparent defeat.

God was disciplining the nations through Nebuchadnezzar, including Judah. However, the discipline would be less severe for those who would humble themselves and submit to God's process. Jerusalem needed not to be laid waste, but only endure a season of difficulty under Nebuchadnezzar's hand until Babylon itself would be judged by God. The Judean people could have lived in their own homes and preserved the city of Jerusalem and the temple from utter destruction by simply embracing God's call to submission and not yielding to the temptation to fight. God's heart was to reduce the extent of His judgment, and this can be seen as He reasoned with the people when He asked, "Why will you die, you and your people, by the sword, by the famine, and by the pestilence, as the LORD has spoken against the nation that will not serve the king of Babylon?" (See verse 13)

As you already know, Jeremiah's prophetic message, being very unpopular and seemingly contrary to the people's view of God, was ignored and resented. The false prophets who spoke a lie in the name of God had tickled the ears of the people and had won their obedience. Jehoiakim, king of Judah, and his son Jehoiachin, rebelled against Nebuchadnezzar. Jehoiakim died and shortly after his son came to power the Babylonians attacked Jerusalem, taking King Jehoiachin and over 10,000 more captives into exile in 597 BC. Zedekiah then became the new ruler, but after only a few years he too rebelled against Nebuchadnezzar. Jerusalem underwent yet another final attack and was utterly destroyed, burned to the ground along with the temple. Some Jews fled to the nearby country of Edom to escape, many died in the fighting, but those left were taken into captivity to Babylon. Nebuchadnezzar took all but the very old, the injured, and the very poor.

The church, like Judah, is coming into a season of discipline and cleansing. I believe that God, through the message of Jeremiah, is warning the church not to engage in militant resistance in the political arena. Doing so may ensure a clamping down on religious freedom by the state, which would in turn cause further exile out of the church. Christianity would slowly move underground. Some could never imagine such a thing happening in the free world, but movement in that direction is already beginning. In a democratic society public opinion is everything. The media perhaps holds the greatest political influence of all. Western culture is slowly turning against the church, and the church is not helping the situation. I can mostly speak as a Canadian watching the social and political movement in our nation.

Certain members of our government are seeking to redefine marriage to include the scenario of homosexual union. Right-wing evangelical Christian organizations are working hard to oppose and defeat the passing of this bill. They claim that this is an attack on marriage and that the church must stand up and fight. Their message is that pastors should be preaching against abortion, homosexuality, and the new threat of euthanasia. These very influential church leaders interpret the lack of involvement and silence from Christians on these issues as an accommodation of sin. There is a pressure from this very loud voice within the Christian evangelical world to be politically militant, as is our duty as Christians in a democratic society.

Much like the many prophets during the time of Jeremiah, these voices are unanimous and sound correct. I thought the same way until God showed me Jeremiah 27. I'm not arguing that we as Christians should redefine morality as culture dictates it to us. Nebuchadnezzar was an evil man. He was responsible for the death of countless numbers of people. He banned prayer being made to any god besides him and built an image of himself for all to worship. Daniel and his three Jewish friends all stood their ground when the State threatened to violate their personal relationship with God. However, is it our business at this point to confront moral issues through legislation and political means?

I maintain that to do so in word, yet not match it with deed, undermines our right to speak. Society is watching the church to see if we live what we preach. How can we condemn activists who we claim are "attacking marriage" when the divorce rate among Christian couples is just as high and adultery is running rampant in the church? Perhaps this is the real attack on marriage. How can we presume to dictate these things to unbelievers without adhering to our own standards?

> Why do you look at the speck in your brother's eye, but do not consider the plank in your own eye? Or how can you say to your brother, 'let me remove the speck from your eye;' and look, a plank is in your own eye? Hypocrite! First remove the plank from your own eye, and then you will see clearly to remove the speck from your brother's eye. (Matthew 7:3-5)

It is because of this general hypocrisy that our resistance towards the social and political powers of the day is being returned with hostility. Conservative evangelicals are concerned that being silent or intimidated, at this point, ensures oppression of religion in Canada. However, I believe that it is the other way around. If we resist this "Nebuchadnezzar," and continue to fight on issues like "gay marriage," we will be solidifying further restriction of religion in this nation.

If our country is morally decaying, perhaps we should stop seeing homosexuals as the cause of this downfall, and take a good look in the mirror as Christians. We are salt and light in this world. Current cultural trends moving towards a degradation of morality are happening only because there isn't a visible kingdom counterculture demonstrating another way of living. As was with Judah and the surrounding nations, there is little difference between the church and the world. I don't believe that protests and petitioning are the appropriate methods to use in this critical moment of our nation's history. It is a time for repentance, fasting, and prayer.

Canadian right-wing Christian political organizations are taking cues from our friends south of the border. The far right of the evangelical movement in the United States has a highly organized campaign to impose biblical law on every aspect of American society. There is a growing emphasis on preaching that it is time to save America—not soul by soul, but election by election.

All the while, with ongoing organized protests, fiery pulpit preaching and political debates, Christians are being seen as aggressive, intolerant, hateful, hypocritical, self-righteous trouble makers. As the church becomes more aggressive and militant in its political cause, this may precipitate a seizing of religious freedom, even if it were only at a social level. If public opinion continues to sway toward hatred of Christians, we may see further exile out of the church. I'm not saying that the church should never speak to the culture about issues of morality. However, the church must gain authority to speak while submitting to God's discipline. The time will come when people and even politicians will hear the wisdom spoken by God's people. I don't believe that time is now.

It is quite interesting to me that Jesus had very little to say about the political power of His day, Rome. The writers of the New Testament launched no bold attack on Rome's policies. The only political comments made were to be faithful to pay your taxes ("Give to Caesar what belongs to Caesar") and to submit to ruling authorities. They understood that the gospel was all about transformation of the heart of individuals, that a society could be changed one soul at a time. "Legislating morality" was not a platform for Jesus or the apostles in their ministry in the good news of Christ.

Paul, an apostle and author of half the New Testament, did not try to dismantle cultural evils, a prime example being slavery. His comments could be interpreted as though he endorsed the idea of a man owning his brother. However, he only encouraged slaves to be Christians, peaceful, and to be good to their masters. This type of behavior is in the spirit of what Jesus taught when He said, "Love your enemies." Perhaps the church can learn from the words and example of Jesus, who carried the message of love, acceptance, and forgiveness to sinners. This is not the message that the homosexual community or the culture in general is receiving from the church.

As far as Western civilization is concerned, perhaps God is waiting patiently until a certain measure of wickedness is reached before he deals with the social evils of our culture. It usually takes God a few hundred years before He judges a nation. He gave the people of Canaan over four hundred years, "for the iniquity of the Amorites is not yet complete." (Genesis 15:16) God may be allowing our nation to be given over to its lust in order for Him to be fully justified when He takes action. Our protests and petitions will do very little to stop this process. I truly believe our attention must be turned to God's dealing with us, as the church. Political engagement at this point serves as a distraction from seeking God and amending our own ways as God's people. Let us submit to God's discipline and stop making enemies with the culture.

DO YOU HAVE TO LEAVE THE BUILDING TOO?

Presently, God has moved millions of Christians out of the organized church to be positioned in society like He did with the early exiles into Babylon. The majority of believers still go to institutional church every Sunday. I know that there are many people, from older believers to new converts, who have received many wonderful things from God through attending church services and being involved in ministries of the church. I am not comfortable dismissing any of these means that have brought life to individuals.

At the same time, please ensure that your reliance and dependence on your church is not a replacement for personal intimacy with God. You must know Him for yourself. Build meaningful relationships with other believers, both young in faith and those more mature than yourself. Find the "true" church within the (institutional) church. God is calling His people to consider their ways and to make sure they are directly connected to Him. These are serious times, not to be taken lightly, or to go on with "business as usual." For there may come a time very soon when all the props will be taken away. If you are not comfortable leaving the organized church at this time, in the near future you may not have much of a choice.

That moment came for Jerusalem. After years of warning and allowing the people to still change the outcome through repentance and submission, God made a firm decision. At a certain point, the option to stop Jerusalem's destruction was taken away from the people. The utter destruction of the city and temple was set in stone and the only choice that was given to its inhabitants was to leave. "Behold, I set before you the way of life and the way of death." (Jeremiah 21:8) Remaining in the city would ensure certain death, and defecting to Babylon would mean survival. God was telling everyone to leave because the fatal end of Jerusalem was unstoppable. "He who remains in this city shall die by the sword, by famine, and by pestilence; but he who goes over to the Chaldeans shall live." (Jeremiah 38:2) Now there was no choice. God had left the building, and so should everyone else who wanted to live.

As I see the direction things are going, there will most likely come a day when it would be unsafe to remain behind the four walls of a church system that is caving in. This is already happening and will continue to progress over the next few decades. As this unravels, multitudes will join those who have already been sent into exile, completely redefining the expression of Christianity in our culture. This exile out of church as we know it is progressing over a period of time in short bursts with intervals in between, much like the Babylonian Exile. Remember, it only took nineteen years back then. How much time does the church have now?

This message is probably as unpopular today as Jeremiah's was in his generation. However, I implore you to ask the Holy Spirit to confirm in your heart whether this message is true. You will know in your heart. May God give you the courage you need to respond to His leading! Don't be afraid to follow Jesus. You know where He is going.

A LETTER TO THE EXILES

Although Jeremiah was primarily a prophetic voice to the city of Jerusalem, he did send a letter to those who had been carried away early into exile. This letter is found in the twenty-ninth chapter of Jeremiah. Feeling like an early exile myself, it brought tremendous encouragement to me. God instilled a peace into my heart through the words of Jeremiah. He showed me how I was to live out here in Babylon.

> Thus says the LORD of hosts, the God of Israel, to all who were carried away captive, whom I have caused to be carried away from Jerusalem to Babylon: "Build houses and dwell in them; plant gardens and eat their fruit. Take wives and beget sons and daughters; and take wives for your sons and give your daughters to husbands, so that they may bear sons and daughters – that you may be increased there, and not diminished. And seek the peace of the city where I have caused you to be carried away captive, and pray to the LORD for it; for in its peace you will have peace."
> (Jeremiah 29:4-7)

It was God who orchestrated the departure of the exiles from their home in Jerusalem. He brought them to this foreign place and culture to cause them to thrive there. The Jews in Babylon would remain in this land for a lifetime. They were in it for the long haul. God was going to restore Jerusalem and the temple once again in a new generation, but this would not begin for at least seventy years. In the meantime, there was a purpose for His people in Babylon.

Settle in Babylon! God wants me to do more than just keep my head above water as an "exile of Judah." I am to flourish here. As a believer, I am amphibious and my life in "Babylon" can be one of blessing and peace. God instructed the exiles to build their homes, be fruitful, have children, grow old and increase in the city God had moved them into.

They were to live their lives out in Babylon and know that God was with them. Paul wrote a similar thought to the church in Thessalonica when he said, "...that you also aspire to lead a quiet life, to mind your own business, and to work with your own hands, as we commanded you, that you may walk properly toward those who are outside, and that you may lack nothing." (1 Thessalonians 4:11, 12)

Jesus is leaving the building to reinvent an old form of Christianity, where His disciples live and act like Jesus out in the real world. People of our culture need to see Christians who don't "go to church," but live quiet lives, who mind their own business, work hard, and walk properly. They live the gospel first before preaching it. All sectors of society are ready and waiting for the many "Daniels" to take their place of influence. The church will have a voice in the days to come. Followers of Jesus will be known as the revealers of mysteries and interpreters of divine revelation. We will emerge like Joseph from his Egyptian prison, like David from the Cave of Adullum. As He did with Cornelius in the first century, God will come close to those seeking Him. God is not expecting these searchers to come to church. He's ready to make a house call. Jesus has left the building.

EPILOGUE

FAREWELL

Well, this is it. We've come to the end. Although I have spent the last several years mostly outside the walls of the church, I have never formally said, "Goodbye." In some ways I have had one foot in and one foot out, as I have continued to speak in churches on Sunday mornings in my travels. However, I must go now. I must find my way out into the world that so desperately needs to see Jesus and hear Jesus through me. I have a house to build and garden to plant. I have to raise my kids and see them find their own place in this world. I am compelled to follow this path to its end.

I imagine for awhile, if you're interested, you may hear or see me talk about the themes contained in the pages of this book. I am willing to further discuss it. I expect a flurry of activity for a season, as readers wrestle through the issues this book raises. I am open to hearing from you and talking through what needs to be said. However, honestly, it has always been my intention for this book to be a farewell message to the institutional church. I am leaving for "Babylon" and I don't imagine I'm ever coming back. I don't know how much longer we will have the opportunity to talk. Perhaps it will be longer than I think. Inevitably, and probably sooner than later, I will be gone. This is what I leave with you.

No Returning

She told me that I was a sinner and that if I tried, 'could do better.
But what is this standard of measure that kicks you when you're down?
She'd say that my faith is fleeting. But I tell you my heart is still beating.
I'm looking for an intimate setting for two.

So I've crossed the line of no returning, though she tried to make me stay.
I hope in time your heart is yearning and I'll see you come my way.

One sip from the cup she was drinking went straight to my head with her thinking.
She had me believe I kept needing to come back for more.
I finally saw through the riddle—no need for someone in the middle.
Hold on, this will hurt just a little. Baby let go.

So I've crossed the line of no returning, though she tried to make me stay.
I hope in time your heart is yearning and I'll see you come my way.

I'm so done with her, who once used prose to cage my rhyme.
Tell me that you're sure, only to change your mind.

A song written by Paul Vieira

ABOUT THE AUTHOR

PAUL VIEIRA is an author and lecturer, seeking to inspire believers to reflect Jesus out in the real world. Paul has much to share about knowing the times that we live in by looking back into biblical history. This is not the first time that God has left the building.

As a teenager, Paul was used by God to sprout a youth ministry that touched hundreds of young people and was critical in setting the direction for Paul's life. Shortly after becoming a lead pastor in his early twenties, Paul began to ask the question, "What church did Jesus go to?" His longing to experience a genuine expression of the original church of Acts compelled Paul to leave institutional forms of church. He now shares life with other lovers of God who often meet around the table, in homes, restaurants, coffee shops or wherever two or three can gather.

Paul is also the director of a discipleship school called the Joppa Experience, located near his home in Canada. He has also made the entire course, which is focused on knowing God and finding Christ throughout all of Scripture, available online at www.joppaonline.com.

Paul's ultimate aspiration is to know and love God. Paul also loves to spend time pursuing another passion, writing and performing music. His joy is his wife and four children.

Visit Paul on the Web at:
www.paulvieira.info and www.jesushasleftthebuilding.com

Printed in the United States
56532LVS00004B/1-108

9 780971 804081